Glasgow Royal Infirmary

A Light thru' the Mirk

Glasgow Royal Infirmary

A Light thru' the Mirk

Henry W Gray

John A Thomson

HWGray

2019

On the front cover: The background is the MacKenzie tartan which was worn by the Glasgow Regiments of the Highland Light Infantry (HLI). The photograph of the Royal Infirmary is from an engraving published 1801 by W Miller, London. The plan was engraved by J.C. Fittler after a drawing by J.C. Nattes.

On the back cover: The background remains the MacKenzie tartan of the front cover. The photograph of the Royal Infirmary was taken in Joseph Lister's male ward but around 1890 and shows a student dresser in short white jacket.

Copyright © 2019 by H W Gray

All rights reserved. This book or any portion thereof may not be reproduced or used in any manner whatsoever without the express written permission of the publisher except for the use of brief quotations in a book review or scholarly journal.

First Printing: 2019

ISBN: 978-0-244-79622-8

H W Gray
Winton Park, East Kilbride
Glasgow, South Lanarkshire, G75 8QW

Dedication

This book is a tribute to all medical, surgical, nursing, scientific, managerial and trades staff who have been part of the Glasgow Royal Infirmary story. It is also a thank you from all patients who have experienced care from the Institution over the centuries.

Oh, the Auld Hoose, the Auld Hoose, What though the wards were wee;
Nae better wark than there was done, we couldna wish to see.

- John Freeland Fergus. M.A, M.D.

Contents

Acknowledgements..8
Foreword...9
Preface...10
Chapter 1: A Hospital Dawns in Glasgow.............................13
Chapter 2: A Royal Infirmary Appears..................................23
Chapter 3: Challenges Overcome..35
Chapter 4: Twin Scourges of Surgery....................................47
Chapter 5: St Mungo's Medical College................................61
Chapter 6: A New Era for Women..75
Chapter 7: Nursing Comes of Age..83
Chapter 8: The Auld Hoose..99
Chapter 9: Electricians Spark Change.................................105
Chapter 10: Redevelopment at Last....................................115
Chapter 11: Medicine and Management.............................135
Chapter 12: Crowd-funding 20th Century Style..................149
Appendix: 165

Acknowledgements

This project has taken considerable time and effort but has also been a valuable learning experience. I would like to thank all who have contributed to this work and for their encouragement. My co-author, John A Thomson has edited with precision and I am grateful for his memory of events and people. Alistair Tough, Head of the Archives Section at the Mitchell Library has been most helpful with advice and direction to the appropriate GRI archives. Andrew McAinsh and Library staff at the Royal College of Physicians and Surgeons of Glasgow have gone out of their way to provide essential data. Craig Richardson of the Department of Medical Illustration, Glasgow Royal Infirmary, has found many of the old images of the hospital for me. George Greig has given me welcome technical encouragement and a fine pipe tune entitled 'Glasgow Royal Infirmary'. A final thanks to my wife for her patience and encouragement and her expert proof-reading.

Henry W Gray
April, 2019

Foreword

My colleague Dr. Gray has asked me to write a foreword to this historical review of the development of the Royal Infirmary of Glasgow.

This is an Institution to which both of us have a great loyalty and affection. We each have had a long association with the hospital, both having spent almost all of our working life in the service of the Institution; each married a "Royal" nurse and each had a parent associated with the hospital; in my case, my mother trained as a nurse (1921-24) and in Dr. Gray's case his father graduated as a doctor from the St Mungo's School of Medicine (1932-1937). This background was useful in obtaining a historical perspective

The majority of the work in putting this publication together, especially the illustrations, was by Dr Gray.

J.A. Thomson
April, 2019

Preface

Glasgow Royal Infirmary (GRI) emerged late in the 18th Century into a city that was expanding and industrialising rapidly. The hospital was built with public funds and relied upon voluntary contributions to survive. GRI followed Edinburgh Royal Infirmary by supplying the local need for reliable health care for working families and the teaching of junior doctors in the art of medicine or surgery. It also supplied the professional training for medical students of the University of Glasgow and the Faculty of Physicians and Surgeons of Glasgow.

A perfect expression of philanthropic giving and endeavour, GRI remained a self-financing institution reliant upon the generosity of the citizens of Glasgow and private sources of funding until the start of the National Health Service in 1948. As it grew to become the largest voluntary hospital in Scotland and the second largest in the United Kingdom, it had to overcome the many difficulties associated with a rising Glasgow City population. For over two Centuries, the Institution has contributed both nationally and internationally in important areas of medicine, surgery, nursing and the medical sciences. Initially the hospital was administered by a committee of lay members serving in a voluntary capacity and staffed by senior medical and surgical staff who were also honorary and unpaid.

Chapter 1, *'A Hospital Dawns in Glasgow'*, sets the scene for the emergence of an Institution where skills and techniques in health care could be concentrated. Scotland has produced more than its share of medical and surgical geniuses and The University of Glasgow and Anderson's University both contributed in large measure.

Chapter 2, *'A Royal Infirmary Appears'*, documents the building of the first GRI. The operation of the early Infirmary and the methods used to seek funding early on are outlined.

Chapter 3, *'Challenges Overcome'*, describes the methods used to face the dual challenges of regular epidemics and a burgeoning population. It concludes with a look at early hospital organization and the need to separate medical and surgical cases by building a new surgical block.

Chapter 4, *'Twin Scourges of Surgery'*, essentially looks at the careers of two of the world's most well-known and venerated surgeons, Joseph Lister and William Macewen. In the chapter, we move from pain relief to sepsis, expand upon antisepsis and finally end with the modern surgical asepsis.

Chapter 5, *'St Mungo's Medical College'* documents the emergence of both the Royal Infirmary School of Medicine and St Mungo's College of Medicine and explores the difficult relationship between GRI and The University of Glasgow.

Chapter 6, *'A New Era for Women'*, documents the many difficulties for women who wanted to be doctors in the 19th Century and the eventual resolution of the problem which required an Act of Parliament.

Chapter 7, *'Nursing Comes of Age'*, is dedicated to the change in nursing from untrained helper and cleaner to highly trained professional brought about by Rebecca Strong and those who followed.

Chapter 8, *'The Auld Hoose'*, presents poetry dedicated to GRI by a former member of medical staff indicating the affection in which the Institution was held.

Chapter 9, *'Electricians Spark Change'*, describes the weeks from discovery to the first practical application of X-rays in GRI. John Macintyre then developed the first hospital X-ray department in the world in his Electrical Department.

Chapter 10, *'Redevelopment at Last'*, provides the background for the enormous task of rebuilding such a well-loved institution. It also highlights the specialist outpatient Dispensaries that appeared mid 19th Century in Glasgow.

Chapter 11, *'Medicine and Management'*, discusses and highlights the enormous input from the Medical Superintendents over GRI's history. It then outlines the groundbreaking advances in tissue transplantation at GRI thanks to the input from plastic surgery. Finally, a quick look at the most junior of the hospital doctors at GRI, the House Officer.

Chapter 12, *'Crowd-funding 20th Century Style'*, outlines many of the methods used by the treasurer of GRI to keep funding adequate until the NHS appeared in July, 1948.

H W Gray
April, 2019

Engraving by John Slezer, 1693 of the Bishop's Castle (centre), Cathedral (right), and University of Glasgow (left)[1]

Chapter 1

A Hospital Dawns in Glasgow

In the dark ages of Scotland, prior to the Reformation of 1560, care of the sick, aged, infirm and dying was undertaken charitably by the established Roman Catholic religious orders in hostels or 'spitles' which appeared to be hostels with some beds for the sick. St Nicholas Hospitle on Kirk Street, close to the Cathedral, was founded in the 15th Century by Bishop Andrew Muirhead and was used as a hospice for men. The Bishops of Glasgow lived in a castle or palace, which was later fortified, beside the Cathedral and built in the late 12th Century. Around 1600, the Trades Alms House or Trades Hospital was built for members of the 14 Incorporated Crafts or

Engraving of the Bishop's Castle (Palace) 1540[2]

Guilds of Glasgow. In 1560, armed citizens and the Trades House militia saved Glasgow Cathedral from the mob's burning and destruction during the Scottish Reformation. In London, St Bartholomew's Hospital appeared in 1123 and remained the only Institution for the sick in that city until the early 1700s.

Following the forceable closure of religious health care provision during the Scottish Reformation, the sick, dying and infirm poor became totally reliant for care upon either secular charities or municipal provision provided by

Protection of Glasgow Cathedral by a citizens militia during the Scottish Reformation of 1560[2]

town councils who did at least subsidise certain physicians and surgeons to attend them. Institutions such as hospitals, asylums and infirmaries emerged under the Scottish Poor Law system that was supported by voluntary financial giving from local philanthropists, special collections, donations, fines and the occasional levy by Parish councils and Kirk Sessions in each area. Although there was a Poor Law in Scotland to deal with poverty and health issues, unlike England, there was no legal provision for relief of destitution. Indeed, evidence strongly suggests that the Kirk Sessions favoured education and provision of schools over poor relief. They promoted personal charitable giving for the poor without local authority involvement and the need for hypothecated taxation by Parish Councils.[3]

Only 'Provand's Lordship', a residence built in 1471 for the chaplain of the nearby Saint Nicholas Hospitle remains on Castle Street to remind us of that era. Saint Nicholas Hospitle had been an almshouse for older men on Kirkgate or as it was known later, Castle Street. A garden for the cultivation of ancient remedies can be seen today at its rear. Physicians in the area were few, some training at the University of Glasgow founded

Provand's Lordship, Castle St[4]

in 1451, but most felt that they had to go abroad to Paris or Leiden after their degree for further training. These individuals with European credentials tended to work in the cities. Barber-surgeons were more numerous and were employed for bloodletting, treatment of wounds and fractures, pulling teeth and the 'cutting' for bladder stones. These 'tradesmen' established the 'Crafts Hospital' or 'Trades Almshouse' for the aged and infirm sited between Rottenrow and St Nicholas Hospitle. Mr **Peter Lowe** who was a co-founder of the Faculty of Physicians and Surgeons of Glasgow was the first surgeon of this institution in 1609. Surgeons separated from barber-surgeons in 1745 into specific trade guilds that were more regulated, and required better training and longer apprenticeship. This permitted them to work in more difficult areas such as amputations and abnormal births.

Mr Peter Lowe[5]

In 1641, Hutcheson's hospital for the elderly and a school for boys was opened in Trongate and was known for the large garden used by its apothecary. Pharmacopoeias of the age contained medicaments of vegetable origin presented in waters, syrups, powders, lozenges, pills, ointments or tinctures. When animal substances appeared, it was usually dried goats blood, urine mixed with salt, millipedes prepared for their formic acid and dried bees. Apothecaries not only provided over-the-counter remedies as chemists do today but also visited the sick at home and were the doctors of last resort for the poor. Surgeon apothecaries or pure apothecaries looked after everyone in the countryside. After an apprenticeship of 5 years to a surgeon or an apothecary which required a training fee, individuals could then set up in practice on their own given the lack of standards for systematic training of the age. There was much irregularity of practice and many charlatans.

Development of Voluntary Hospitals in Scotland

With the 18th Century came the Union of Parliaments and its associated industrial developments with the resulting population growth in cities. The population of London burgeoned and five voluntary general hospitals appeared namely the Westminster (1719), Guy's (1721), St George's (1733), The London Infirmary (1740) and The Middlesex (1745). Due to Scotland's trade with the United States, and as a result of highland clearances, Glasgow's population grew

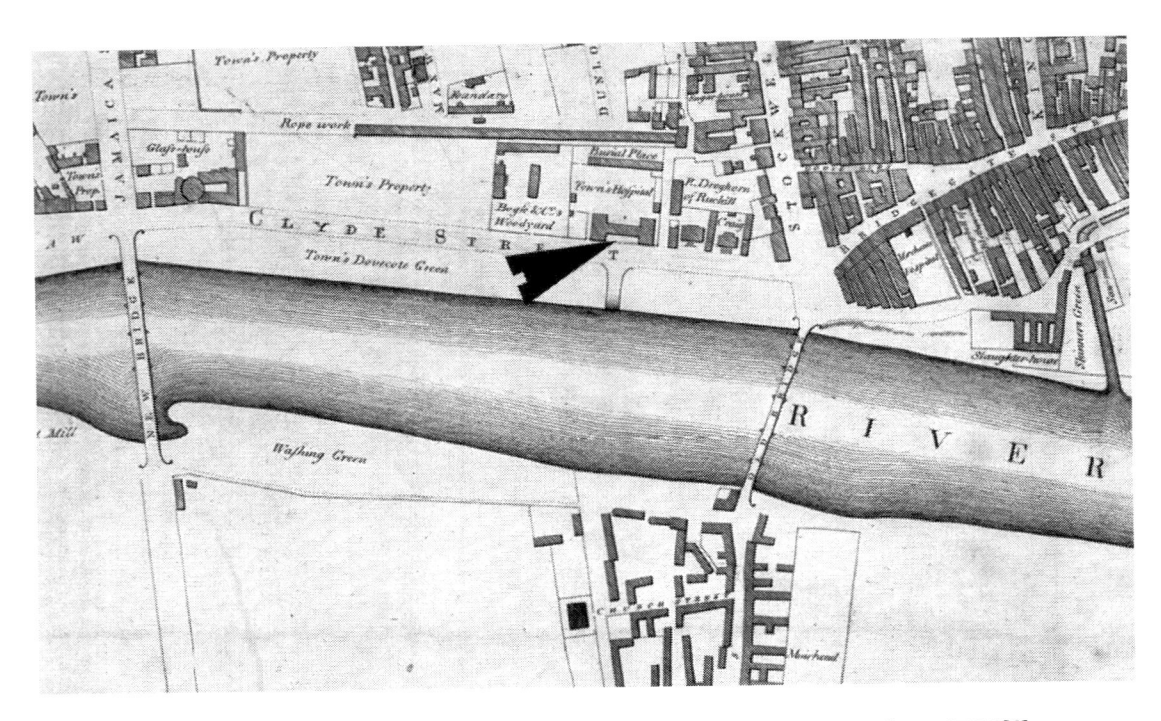

Town's Hospital on Clyde St. Map by John MacCarthur 1778[6]

from 14,000 in 1712 to 83,000 in 1801 and 200,000 in 1830. Later, it would be the lingering effects of the Irish potato famines in the 1840s-50s that continued to swell the numbers in the city and it's suburbs. In the 18th Century, the 'Voluntary Hospital Movement', which was seen so prominently in London, appeared also in Scotland to provide advice, care for, and treat those in work who were unable to afford health care in the community. Medical and surgical staff in those special voluntary Institutions worked a few hours each day, held honorary positions only and were unsalaried. This work, however, permitted them access to the developing middle class and professional men who could afford health care and, in particular, the really wealthy families in the community. It was this wealthy group who increasingly subscribed to the voluntary hospital's upkeep. In the period from 1729 to 1782, the Crown granted Royal Charters to Edinburgh (1729), Aberdeen (1739), Montrose (1782) and Paisley (1786) for the development of hospitals, which in Scotland were called Royal Infirmaries, and not Hospitals. They were built ostensibly for the care of the working poor who could not afford private physicians to treat members of the family at home[7] and were funded by public subscription.

The first civic response in Glasgow, which had more poverty, disease, beggars and destitution than Edinburgh, was to build **Town's Hospital and**

Poorhouse[8] that opened in 1733 close to the river Clyde. This institution was managed and maintained by the Provost of Glasgow assisted by directors elected by the town council, the General Session representing the Church in each Parish, the Merchants' Guild and the Incorporated Trades (Producer's Guild) who contributed in agreed proportions. It provided relief, food and education for the destitute, infirm, widows and orphans using a workhouse model. Beds for the sick were added a few years later in an Infirmary Block that accommodated the mentally ill in its basement. Medical provision was courtesy of attending physicians and surgeons from the Faculty of Physicians and Surgeons of Glasgow (FPSG). The FPSG had been founded by Royal Charter from King James the 6th of Scotland in 1599 by Mr **Peter Lowe** (surgeon) and Dr **Robert Hamilton** (physician). The charter established the Faculty in law as a regulator of medical and particularly surgical qualifications and licensing of said practitioners for work in the West of Scotland. In addition, the charter went on to outline the legal power to inspect drugs where it mentioned **William Spang**, an apothecary, and tasked the Faculty to visit the poor on a regular basis without fee. This was the first sign in Scotland of a medical interest in public health. Peter Lowe had been an Ambassador for Scotland abroad and an experienced surgeon in France for many years. He had trained at the community of St-Côme in Paris and brought back to Glasgow in the 1590s, a level of surgical expertise unrivalled among his peers in the UK. His published work remains a testimony to this.[9]

Town's Hospital and Poorhouse[2]

Robert Hamilton[5]

William Spang[5]

The addition of the Infirmary beds into Town's Hospital permitted some teaching for medical students of the University of Glasgow and the apprentices of local surgeons of the FPSG who were more numerous. **William Cullen** who was Professor of Medicine from 1751 to 1756 at the University of Glasgow and lectured in English, not Latin, was one of the teachers found in Town's Hospital from 1747 and it was he who advocated the training of doctors in scientific

William Cullen FRS[10]

subjects such as chemistry. He himself was an apothecary as well as a surgeon and had a huge number of 'medicines' at his disposal from his druggist in Hamilton where he practiced.[3] He advocated inoculation against smallpox and this was quite effective.

Later in 1796, **Edward Jenner** discovered vaccination and smallpox became less of a problem in Scotland. One year after opening, 61 old people and 90 children were resident in Town's Hospital. It is not clear when it closed but it is likely to have been after GRI opened in 1794. Residents were apparently transferred to the new Glasgow City Poorhouse on Parliamentary Road. **Joseph Black** followed Cullen as Professor of Medicine and Chemistry at the University of Glasgow until 1766 when he left for Edinburgh. His laboratory research was extraordinarily fruitful with discoveries of the element magnesium, the gas carbon dioxide, and the concepts of latent heat and specific heat.

Joseph Black MD. FRSE.

William Hunter from Long Calderwood, East Kilbride, was a pupil of Cullen's when he worked in Hamilton and, from him, learned the importance of practical demonstration to illustrate major points during teaching. After studies at the University of Glasgow and abroad, he went to London to be a pupil in midwifery with **William Smellie**, who was a fellow Scot in London, performing ground-breaking work on the gravid uterus. By developing his own extra mural school of midwifery and anatomy in the Capital in the 1740s at Great Windmill Street, Hunter completely changed how these subjects were taught in the United Kingdom and became the leading obstetrician in London and manmidwife to Royalty. William Hunter died in 1783 and bequeathed his museum to the University of Glasgow. This museum continues to exhibit his specimens to this day.

William Hunter FRS by Sir Joshua Reynolds

John Hunter, William's younger brother, had a basic education only and, aged 20, followed his brother to London in 1748. William trained him in anatomical dissection and in return, he helped his brother with the dissections for display in William's anatomical school. Within a short time, John showed such skill and aptitude that he began to teach in his brother's school. He trained in the art of surgery at the Chelsea and St Bartholomew's Hospitals then spent 3 years as an army surgeon. During all this time, his curiosity, observation and insight helped him develop a scientific method of investigation in medicine and surgery that relied on proof by trial and experiment. John became the first to use anatomy and particularly the post mortem examination as a corrective diagnostic tool in medicine and became a leader in the new investigative medical science. His interests extended beyond medicine with his mastery of comparative anatomy. John Hunter, an irascible Scot, died in 1793 and left an

John Hunter FRS by Sir Joshua Reynolds

John (L) and William (R) Hunter Medals in Physiology and Surgery, University of Glasgow, 1963-4[11]

enduring legacy of achievement, surprising for one so humbly born. On his death, he gifted his extensive museum to the Royal College of Surgeons of England in London.

John Anderson, was Professor of Natural Philosophy at the University of Glasgow from 1757 and an important academic who stayed in Scotland to influence medical training. In 1796, he bequeathed money on his death to found Anderson's University which later became a College in 1877. This excellent educational establishment for scientific subjects rivalled the University of Glasgow and, unusually for its time, admitted women for study. Anderson's College Medical School provided excellent training for aspiring physicians and surgeons in anatomy and in the science of medicine and was a training ground for aspiring

John Anderson FRS.FRSE by William Cochrane [12]

lecturers and Professors at the University of Glasgow. There were 700 College students matriculated in 1830. Medical training was first rate and as an extra mural medical school, was eventually to play an important role in the undergraduate training of doctors at Glasgow Royal Infirmary (GRI). By 1840, Anderson's University had twice as many medical students enrolled as the University of Glasgow. It's scientific departments eventually amalgamated with other Institutions to become the Glasgow Technical College in 1886, and the Royal Glasgow Technical College in 1912. This College became the University of Strathclyde[13] in the early 1960s. The University of Strathclyde maintained scientific and medical links with GRI from its inauguration in the early 1960s. This cooperation, which followed four main themes, was encouraged and fostered by

Anderson's University, George St[14]

it's first Principal, Sir **Samuel (Sam) Curran** who had invented the scintillation counter while a member of the Manhattan Project. The first theme was isotopes in medicine. Curran had provided the then Dr **Edward McGirr** of the GRI Academic Department of Medicine with his first radioactive counting equipment in the early 1950s. McGirr went on to major discoveries in the realm of thyroid disease and genetics. The second theme was in bioengineering and prosthetics. Professor **Thomas (Tom) Gibson,** who was a plastic surgeon at GRI, co-founded the Bioengineering Unit at the University of Strathclyde in 1963 with Professor **Robert M Kenedi** thanks to a large grant from the British Medical Research Council. This followed upon work by Gibson and **Peter Medawar** on the causes of rejection of transplanted tissue. The third theme was that of clinical pharmacology. In the mid 1970s, Professor **David H Lawson**, physician and clinical pharmacologist at GRI joined the Pharmacy School for teaching and research purposes. The fourth theme was the health of the University's students. In early 1961, Professor **William (Bill) Manderson**, physician at GRI and Dr **Astor B Sclare**, senior psychiatrist from the Eastern District Hospital, began a part-time health service for the students within the Royal College of Technology building. In 1964, the service changed location to Livingstone Tower and was run as the Student Health Service of the University of Strathclyde. It continued to be led on a part-time basis from 1964 to 2012 by, in succession, Professor Bill Manderson, Professor **Iain T Boyle** and Dr **Henry W Gray**, physicians at GRI.

Sir Sam Curran

Bill Manderson

References

[1]. Engraving of the Cathedral, Bishop's Palace and University, Glasgow *https://en.wikipedia.org/wiki/Glasgow_Cathedral.html* - last accessed March 2019

[2]. Images courtesy of Alistair Tough, Archive Department, Mitchell Library, Glasgow, 2018.

[3]. The Healers: A History of Medicine in Scotland. David Hamilton. 1981.

[4]. Image reproduced courtesy of Glasgow Museums

[5]. Images courtesy of Andrew McAinsh and the Royal College of Physicians of Glasgow archive, 2018.

[6]. Reproduced with the permission of the National Library of Scotland *https://auth.nls.uk/eresources/* - last accessed March 2019

[7]. A Medical History of Scotland. John D Comrie, 2nd edition. Published by the Wellcome Historical Medical Museum, 1932. *http://www.electricscotland.com/history/medical/scottishmedicine02.pdf* - last accessed March 2019

[8]. Town's Hospital and Poorhouse *http://www.workhouses.org.uk/Glasgow/* - last accessed March 2019

[9]. Physicians and Surgeons in Glasgow: The History of the Royal College of Physicians and Surgeons of Glasgow, 1599 – 1858. Johanna Geyer – Kordesch and Fiona MacDonald, The Hambledon Press, 1999.

[10]. William Cullen engraving from Robert Chambers and Thomas Thomson, A Biographical Dictionary of Eminent Scotsmen in Four Volumes, vol 2, 1855.

[11]. Dr Henry W Gray, personal reflection and collection.

[12]. Image courtesy of Andersonian Library, The University of Strathclyde.

[13]. The Shaping of the Medical Profession. The History of the Royal College of Physicians and Surgeons of Glasgow, 1858-1999. Andrew Hull and Johanna Geyer-Kordesch, The Hambledon Press, 1999.

[14]. A Medical History of Scotland. John D Comrie, 2nd edition. Published by the Wellcome Historical Medical Museum, 1932. *http://www.electricscotland.com/history/medical/scottishmedicine02.pdf*

Chapter 2

The Royal Infirmary Appears

The continued rapid growth in the population of Glasgow was linked to the Highland Clearances but mainly resulted from the industrial revolution which required workers to operate the industrial machines that were appearing everywhere. The Royal Infirmary of Edinburgh not only provided institutional care for these workers in Edinburgh city but was also successful as a teaching hospital linked to the University of Edinburgh. The University of Glasgow noticed this as did the local factory and mill owners who were most in need of a healthy workforce. There was also a political aspect to the need for advanced healthcare for the working poor. This was the time of the French Revolution and the new social and political ideology from France lent credence to worries of a French invasion. Insurrection was a constant fear for the governing and upper classes and so it was in their interest to support the 'common weal' and in particular, the health of their workers.

Professor George Jardine[1]

On 5th June 1787, a meeting of those interested in the foundation of a hospital in Glasgow met with **George Jardine**, Professor of Logic and **Alexander**

Print of The University of Glasgow on High Street (College of Glasgow). Blackfriars Church on the (R)[2]

Stevenson, Professor of Medicine at the University of Glasgow situated in High Street. Key groups who provided essential support included leading Glasgow merchants, merchant and trade guilds and the Faculty of Physicians and Surgeons (FPSG). Within 2 weeks of that meeting, a committee had formed including the President of the FPSG and plans were laid for 'the relief of indigent persons labouring under poverty and disease'. The first legacy was £300 from the will of one **James Coulter** who died in 1789 and this did much to encourage the team. They had to seek a Royal Charter in 1791 and began to organise for the collection of subscriptions from the working poor and the middle classes. All legal fees incurred by this activity were also gifted to the Infirmary building. In 1792, a Royal Charter was granted by the Crown, to establish a Royal Infirmary in Glasgow providing charitable care for the working needy of the city. The choice of site was driven by cost, proximity to water and good drainage. It was also important that the Infirmary was close to the University of Glasgow Medical School, which was within the 'Old College' on High Street, to enable undergraduate clinical teaching.

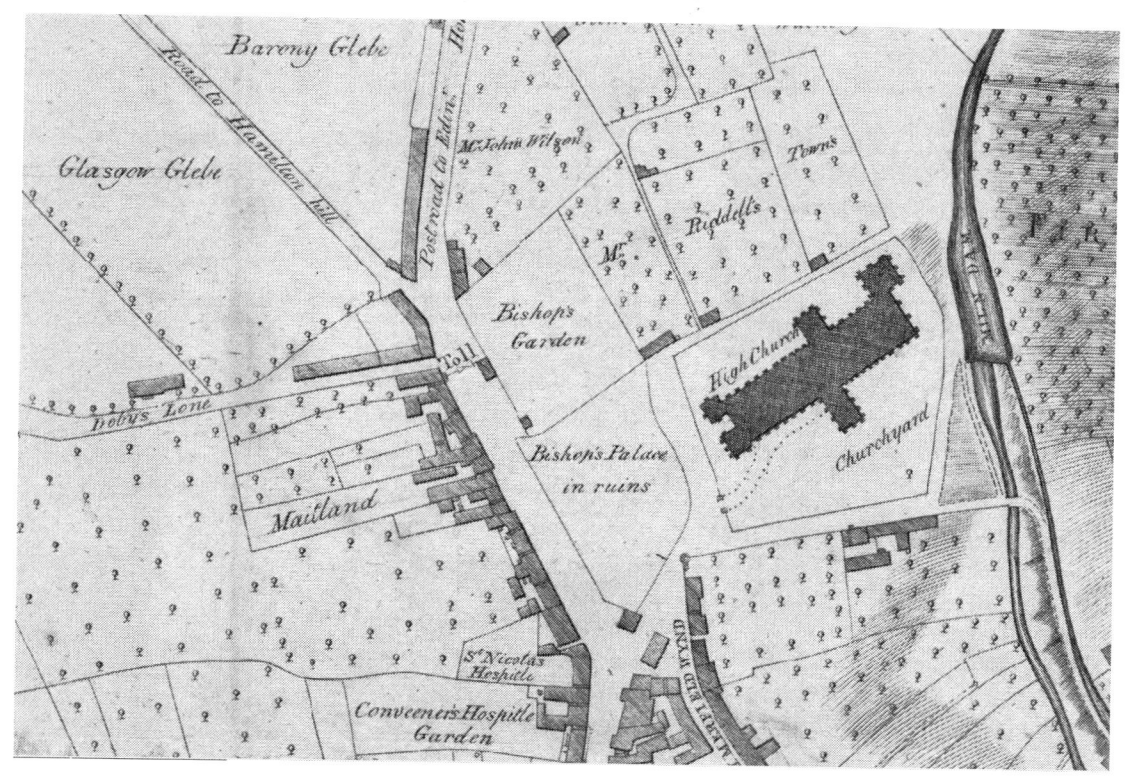

Map of Cathedral area 1778 by John MacCarthur[31]

The first architect to be approached and then appointed was one **William Blackburn** who had a practice in London. On the way to Glasgow to discuss his ideas with the committee, he died suddenly at Preston and his Group declined to take the plans further. This was a blow to the development committee but it so happened that **Robert Adam**, a Scottish architect and designer based in London, was at that specific time overseeing the construction of his design for the new 'Trades House' in Glassford Street in Glasgow. He was eventually persuaded by the team to take over

Trades House of Glasgow by Robert Adam FRS. FRSE.

from Blackburn at short notice and began working on his own design. With an eye to the cost of such an endeavour, the committee asked Adam to build the Infirmary in phases to permit revenue collection. Adam produced a design in 1791 that was ambitious with an impressive principle elevation that reflected the civic pride in the project. There may also have been some underlying competition with Edinburgh Royal Infirmary since that had been designed and built by his father, **William Adam** in 1732. Robert Adam clearly used his own tried and tested design off the shelf given the similarities between the Trades House facade and that of the GRI.

Robert Adam, FRS. FRSE, Architect

Royal Infirmary to be Built on Site of Bishop's Castle, West of the Cathedral of St Mungo[4]

Adam's first design was declined by the development committee because of cost (£8725) so he reduced it to £7185 10s and this was accepted. It was subsequently discovered in 1910 during demolition and rebuilding that Adam had

26

compromised by using wood as a substitute for stone internally to reduce cost. Crown property leased to the Earl of Dundonald and close to the Glasgow Cathedral was chosen as the perfect site for construction. This was the area where the Roman Catholic Church and hierarchy had established the grand, former Archbishop's Castle and yard in the 13th Century until they left in 1560. Professor Jardine persuaded the Lords of His Majesty's Treasury and Barons of the Exchequer to grant the land for the Hospital. This site was ideal since there were two Scotch acres (two thirds of the Imperial acre) available and suitable for the Infirmary. There was also a space for a garden for ambulant patients. It was just up High Street from the University of Glasgow (Old College) and also in proximity to the largest cemetery in Scotland which eventually became the Glasgow Necropolis in 1835.[6] By the 18th Century, the Bishop's Castle site had become a derelict ruin which provided stone for local masons to use for any new building construction in the area. It had to be cleared before building could start but this exercise provided the clerk of works with much of the stone he required for the hospital building. The site was high above the city, and was well aired since buildings could not surround it. There was a sufficient supply of good water from wells within the castle and grounds, and for back up, the Monkland canal was near. A public washing green was available at the Molindinar Burn nearby. However, a water pipe did require to be laid from the Monkland Canal to GRI in 1794 and the water filtered before use. Some decades later, the Glasgow Water Works provided fresh water from Loch Katrine.

Print of University Courtyard on High Street. The 'Old College', 1791[5]

Robert Adam produced a 4 storey and basement building for 136 beds, eight wards with 17 beds each, within the financial means of the good people and Institutions of Glasgow albeit, by compromising on its longevity by the use of wood internally. In May 1792, the Lord Provost assisted by **James Adam**, architect, Robert Adam's brother and Messrs **Morrison and Burns**, Contractors, laid the foundation stone of the Royal. A Benediction was then pronounced over the stone. *"May the Grand Architect of the Universe grant a blessing on this foundation stone and may he enable us to raise a superstructure upon it which shall prove a house of refuge and consolation to the diseased poor of this city and neighbourhood"*.[7] This prayer was effectively the mission statement of the founding fathers of GRI. Unfortunately, Robert Adam died in 1792 before his plan was completed so it was brother James who supervised the construction that proceeded remarkably quickly and it was he who was present at the opening of Glasgow Royal Infirmary (GRI) on 8th December 1794. James Adam himself died at home in London in 1794, the year that patients were first admitted to the Infirmary. He left one of the most impressive buildings imaginable for use by all of the citizens of Glasgow, rich and poor.

Glasgow Royal Infirmary in 1812 by Chapman[4]

The Royal Infirmary in Operation

The main facade of GRI was classical in appearance and symmetrical with a broad central entrance bay. Above that entrance was the typical Adam style arched tripartite window set within a pediment with coupled columns. An impressive dome was placed in the centre and the whole building endeavour actually cost £9,000. Jardine, an able administrator and said to be consumed by zeal and philanthropy, chaired the Board of Management committee for another 20 years.

Engraving of GRI from the Kirkgate. The Building with a Steeple is the Trades Hospital, 1800[4]

Robert Cleghorn, past president of the FPSG and physician to the GRI was also on the Board as was **David Dale** the industrialist and philanthropist who founded the New Lanark Community. The President of the FPSG and Professors of Medicine and Surgery of the University were on the Board ex-officio. Surgery and medicine were in the same building with a large operating theatre beneath the huge dome. It held 200 students and apprentices who would gather there for their clinical tuition in surgery. The theatre became a chapel every Sunday for early morning church services so it was no real surprise

Permanent Chapel beneath the Dome from 1861[4]

that it became a permanent chapel for the Infirmary when the Lister surgical Block opened 60 years later. Students would come for teaching in the required clinical skills from the University on High Street or from the FPSG.

The sick-poor could receive free advice from attending physicians and surgeons in the 'waiting room' at GRI (forerunner of the outpatient 'Dispensary' and later still, the 'Casualty/Accident and Emergency') that was in the vestibule of the Adam building and in the first year, had seen 3,000 individuals. In the 50th Annual Report of 1844, this number had risen to between 4,000 and 5,000 per annum. The more sick and therefore less fortunate would have required 'lines of admission' from GRI subscribers which guaranteed admission. Wards were opened incrementally when funds for equipment became available. In the

Adam Building Logo for GRI Annual Reports by B Massley Snr[41]

first year, 276 were admitted. In 1796, a report went to the contributors that they were 'not exempt from the ills of life'. It went on that 'time may come when assistance and sympathy of others may be more useful and comfortable than all their current possessions'. In the annual report of that year, the Managers acknowledged 'the faithful and useful labours of medical gentlemen who, leaving their business 2 hours each day, employ their time in the painful and fatiguing labours of the Royal Infirmary'. The most junior physicians and surgeons (clerks) were not resident initially but by 1796 it was decided that they were required to stay within the premises and were charged £30 for the privilege of full board. The Apothecary was tasked with collection of student fees and the money paid by patients. Together, the Matron and the Apothecary checked that the gates were locked each night at 10pm and that no member of the team was absent without leave. By arrangement with the FPSG, two attending part-time physicians, Drs **Hope** and **Cleghorn**, provided the medical expertise and were given permission to lecture in 1794. Four surgeons in rotation provided the surgical expertise and Mr **John Burns** began giving lectures in Surgery in 1797. Surgery was very primitive given the lack of anaesthesia and almost inevitability of post-operative infection. In 1800, for example, there were only 41 operations on 803 patients and by 1840, only 120 operations on 5185 patients.[7] In November 1797, two sedan chairs were purchased to convey fever patients to hospital in order to prevent public infection. This was the beginning of an ambulance service in Glasgow. Initially, one of the surgeon clerks was the apothecary (dispensing pharmacist) but in 1800, **John Allan** was appointed to provide, prepare, and dispense medicine but also to take care of the leeches. The University naturally wanted their own medical professors to provide lectures at GRI for medical trainees. However, the FPSG guarded its monopoly on lecturing resolutely and it remained a bone of contention between both organisations until 1907-11 when the Muirhead Trust fortunately intervened to make the University an equal partner with FPSG in medical/surgical undergraduate training at GRI.

The Royal Seeks it's Own Funding

As a voluntary hospital from the day that the first stone was laid, GRI had to raise its own capital and running costs but this provided fewer difficulties than one might expect because Glasgow was a generous city. There was strong financial support from the Faculty of Physicians and Surgeons of Glasgow and the University contributed a generous £500 to the construction. In 1802, the First Regiment of Glasgow Volunteers disbanded and gifted £1200 to the Infirmary. Inevitably, however, GRI's fortunes became inextricably linked to the economic

> On the 17th November last, the Rev. JOHN BOWER, minister of Old Monkland, paid to the Treasurer of the Glasgow Royal Infirmary, 34l. 15s. 6d. being subscriptions from several well disposed people, inhabitants of said parish, and which, with sundry collections formerly paid, makes up the sum of 50l. Sterling for said parish.

Subscriptions Sought Widely, Caledonian Mercury, 1806[9]

health of Glasgow's trade and industry. At the time, Glasgow was a major port. Shipbuilding had developed as had light and heavy engineering which were all labour intensive.[8] The Annual Report of GRI at the beginning of the year reflected the financial struggles, triumphs, and failures of which medical, surgical and nursing staff were largely unaware. Throughout this early time, the innovative methods used by GRI Board of Management to seek financial support from Glasgow and the surrounding area were of the greatest importance. There were three broad classes of revenue. Firstly, there was *conditional income* where money was received for a

> **Advertisements.**
>
> GLASGOW ROYAL INFIRMARY.—The DIRECTORS respectfully request of those Gentlemen who have kindly undertaken the charge of the ANNUAL SUBSCRIPTION PAPERS, that they will proceed, with all possible despatch, to finish the Collection in their respective Districts, as many Families will shortly leave town, and, consequently, the Funds of the Institution may suffer from farther delay. It is expected, that all the Subscription Papers be with Mr. LUMSDEN, the Treasurer, by the middle of May.

Time for the Collection of Subscriptions, The Glasgow Herald, 1840[4]

service that the Infirmary could supply to the donor. Examples were the regular subscriptions from the middle classes and working families that provided access to a bed in the hospital when required. Other examples were the charging of patients who could pay for their board such as the soldiers billeted locally, and the contributions from local merchants or factory owners. Church congregations

> In conveying this expression of grateful feeling to Mr. Alston, the Directors are naturally led to notice the valuable service performed to the Institution by those gentlemen who dividing the town into districts, have taken the trouble to assist in collecting the Annual Subscriptions. Without the aid of these gentlemen the Directors are aware the Annual Subscriptions would have been considerably less than they are. And for these important services the Directors request that these gentlemen will receive their sincere thanks. For all other acts of kindness done to the Institution, the Directors now offer their acknowledgments;

Grateful Thanks to collectors of Annual Subscriptions, The Glasgow Herald, 1827[9]

also paid for health care access for their employees or the parishioners. Conditional income was also raised from the sale of student 'tickets' to attend wards and theatres for teaching and practical experience and finally, as the resident clerk's board and lodging. Secondly, there were the free gifts where there was *no condition* or restriction and this included legacies from estates, donations from the wealthy middle class, gifts of small or large sums, fines, special collections after sermons relating to ministry, exhibitions and lectures by medical staff, and money raised from specific social events or publications. This included the Charity Box that was kept in full view in the Adam building (The Auld Hoose). Finally there was *hospital income* itself derived from lands, rents from houses that the hospital had been gifted, and the interest on all capital, Bonds or accumulated stock invested in the City. The GRI was never wealthy in the final category since most funding was used to improve the premises. Management always announced financial gifts, legacies and the names of collectors in the local newspapers to encourage others to take up the challenge. In 1810, fees paid by students for tuition in wards or in lectures amounted to over £200. In the early days, those individuals in the community who paid a lump sum of £10 or an annual subscription of 1 guinea (£1.10) were entitled to recommend one patient each year to be admitted to GRI for treatment. Those, such as the landed gentry, who were able to provide a higher donation, could recommend more individuals to the hospital for admission and treatment.

The late Miss Maxwell of Ferguslie, bequeathed a legacy of £50 to the Glasgow Royal Infirmary, which has been paid to the treasurer by the trustees acting under her settlement.

Legacy for GRI Announced in The Perthshire Courier, 1816[9]

GRI Income from Annual Accounts, The Glasgow Herald, 1849[9]

It is clear from the accounts of the era that personal subscriptions to GRI were the most important source of income for running costs. As time progressed and industrialisation continued, the contributions from employees would increase as would the contributions from employers in mines, factories, foundries and mills. GRI fund raising would continue to adapt to changing circumstances and would eventually spread its reach into the West of Scotland and beyond. Survival of the Institution depended upon the creative instincts of GRI Administration and the generosity of the citizens of Glasgow and its environs.

References

[1]. Image courtesy of The Hunterian, University of Glasgow, 2018.

[2]. Images courtesy of Andrew McAinsh and the Royal College of Physicians of Glasgow archive, 2018.

[3]. Reproduced with the permission of the National Library of Scotland *http://www.maps.nls.uk/index.html*

[4]. Images courtesy of Alistair Tough, Archive Department, Mitchell Library, Glasgow, 2018.

[5]. Old Glasgow: The place and the people. Andrew MacGeorge, 3rd edition, 1888.

[6]. The Royal: The History of Glasgow Royal Infirmary 1794 – 1994. Jacqueline Jenkinson, Michael Moss and Iain Russell. 1994.

[7]. History of the Glasgow Royal Infirmary. Dr Moses Steven Buchanan, Glasgow, 1832. – Courtesy of Mr Alistair Tough, Archive Department, Mitchell Library, Glasgow.

[8]. Glasgow Works: An account of the economy of the city. Michael Boulton-Jones, 2009. ISBN: 978-1-905553-35-8. Published by Dolman Scott.

[9]. Images courtesy of the British Newspaper Archive.

Chapter 3

Challenges Overcome

The overall success of strategies for income generation from the public was a relief for the Board of Management although the twin problems of population explosion and epidemic fever just had to be faced. New beds were essential to cope with demand within a short space of twenty years – but where? The initial thought was to add to the current bed complement by the addition of a North Block joined to the combined East and West Blocks of GRI. Extra money was sought from the public and using the experience gained over 20 years of fund raising, the results were gratifying. This allowed the addition of a further 72 beds in 1815 with the construction of a North Block in sympathy with the original Adam construction.

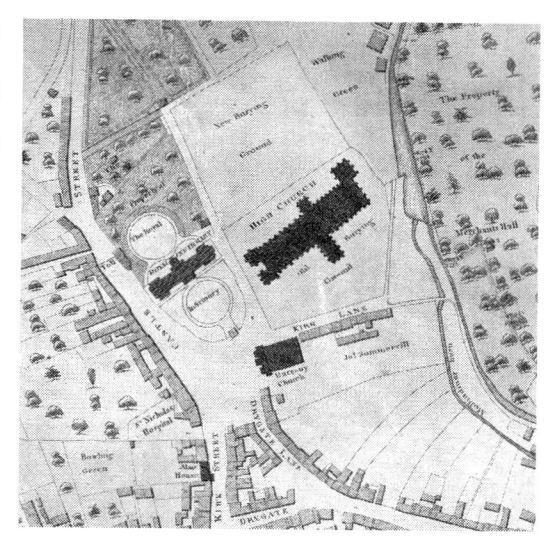

Adam Block in 1807 with St Nicholas Hospitle and Trades Almshouse on Kirk Street. Peter Fleming, 1807[1]

Another stimulus to the plan for a North Block was the increasing use of the Manager's offices for the beds of paying patients. This private facility provided welcome conditional income. The lessons learned would facilitate the building of an auxiliary hospital at Canniesburn a century later which also contained new private beds. The North Block cost the sum of £4000 in total. The four new wards were each smaller than the original Adam wards, (18 beds), and were built at a

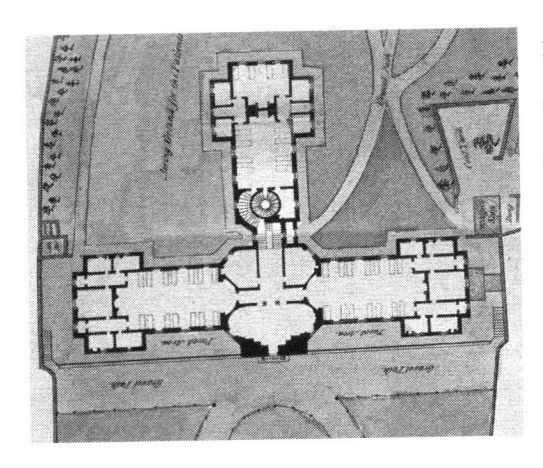

Adam Block with New North Block, 1815[2]

right angle to the centre North face of the original Adam building and directly into the courtyard. Interestingly, the spiral staircase providing access to the different levels of the North Block produced a deep-toned note like a great organ pipe during gales originating from the South West.

At this point in time, staff who had been appointed to GRI began to change the face of medicine and surgery in the United Kingdom and beyond. One of the first of these was **Andrew Buchanan** who became consultant surgeon to GRI in the 1820s after training in Glasgow, Edinburgh and Paris. He was an inquisitive clinician with a keen mind who was really the first to establish GRI as a centre for medical research. Buchanan had many talents teaching Materia Medica at the Andersonian Institute, dabbling in biochemistry and being a founder of the Glasgow Skin Dispensary. He went on to establish the Glasgow Medical Journal in 1828 as a forum for local research and appeared to like the rough and tumble of debate, particularly when it related to the political issues of the day in Glasgow. He apparently lacked tact as an editor and was not popular with his students. This journal eventually merged with the Edinburgh Medical Journal in 1956 to be known as 'The Scottish Medical Journal'. Buchanan is remembered for his research and in particular his interest in the blood and its coagulation. He noted that there was a soluble component of blood and body fluids that coagulated in contact with serum of blood already coagulated. He called this a 'fibrinoplastic' substance that we now know as thrombin. That soluble component of blood he

Andrew Buchanan

called 'fibrinogen'. Buchanan was the first Regius Professor of the Institute of Medicine (later called Physiology) at the University of Glasgow from 1839 to 1876 and in 1879, became President of the FPSG.

Epidemic Fever

The Glasgow scene in the early 19th Century was punctuated by recurrent epidemics of cholera, typhus and enteric fevers that impacted hugely and of necessity upon the use of beds at the new hospital. Fever patients were admitted in an attempt to control the spread of the epidemic within the city. This became a real capacity issue and in 1827, wooden huts were erected in the grounds to act as overflow specifically for the fever cases. Since these patients were admitted as emergencies to safeguard the public health, they were non-payers and so during epidemics, the finances of the hospital suffered and could become critical quite quickly. At times like these, special appeals by the Board were required. Those would be published in The Herald newspaper in Glasgow and in other surrounding newspapers to maintain Institutional solvency. Each time, the people of the West of Scotland, the local Trades Guilds and multiple congregations of Glasgow rose to the challenge.

Dr Robert Perry by Sir Daniel Macnee[3]

It was during this period that an eminent physician at GRI, Dr **Robert Perry**, first pointed out the distinction between typhus and typhoid. Up until then, these conditions were considered medically indistinguishable which contributed to their spread in the community. Perry saw that they required different treatment and different preventative action by public health authorities. In 1836, he published this seminal work in the Edinburgh Medical Journal[4] showing conclusively that those epidemics were related and confined

Slums off High Street by Thomas Annan[5]

to areas of the city where squalor and appalling poverty were the norm. He used maps to show where the fevers struck most severely and published the influential *'Facts and Observations on the Sanitary State of Glasgow'* in 1844. This was the method used later by **John Snow** to show the distribution of cholera around a single water well on Broad Street in Soho, London. Perry may have been the first to use epidemiological techniques in Glasgow.[4] It was around this time in 1825 that the Lock Hospital opened on 41 Rottenrow for the specific treatment of venereal diseases and only closed when the NHS appeared in 1948.

Professor **William Pultoney Allison**, Chair of Medicine at Edinburgh, argued against the General Assembly concerning his belief that hypothecated taxation for the relief of the poor, as practiced in England, was a necessity in Scotland. He showed persuasively that the English system eliminated beggars and reduced destitution that was so prevalent in Scotland and successfully linked it with epidemics of infectious disease. Allison's recommendations were accepted and the new Poor Law for Scotland was passed in 1845. This taxation enabled Parochial Boards to fund the building of fever hospitals, and in 1865, **Parliamentary Road Fever Hospital** was opened followed by **Belvidere Municipal Fever Hospital** in 1874 to accommodate infectious disease in Glasgow.[6]

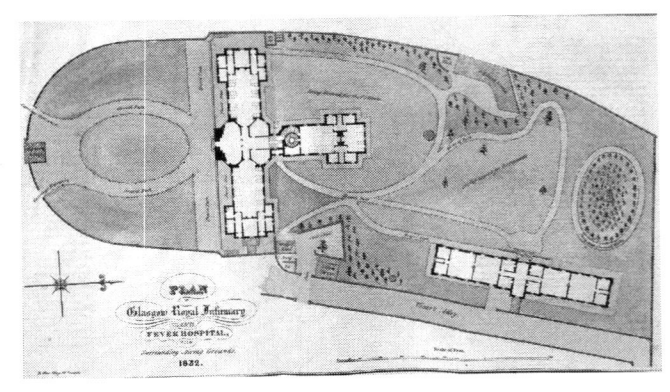

1832 drawing proposing a 220 bed fever hospital onto the original extended Adam Block[2]

Fever cases in the city were so numerous in 1831 that 213 out of 374 beds, including the wards in wooden huts for 80 beds, were occupied by fever cases. GRI Managers responded to the emergency by renting an unused cotton mill in

Albion Street and fitted it with 135 beds to cope with the overflow of cholera cases. Money was eventually found by appeal to build a new West-facing fever hospital for GRI designed by **George Murray** at a right angle to the Adam building and separate from it. This opened in 1834 providing a further 220 beds and cost £8,292.9s.3d. The huts, however, became a permanent feature and when there were low numbers of infectious diseases around, they were used for surgical patients. It was always thought that cases from the huts recovered better because of the better ventilation. In 1842, it was decided that the detached Fever Hospital should become linked to the main Infirmary by a new building extension containing a large lecture theatre, waiting room, outpatient dispensary, inspection room and a pathological museum for all teaching purposes.

West Facade of Fever Block into Courtyard 1870[5]

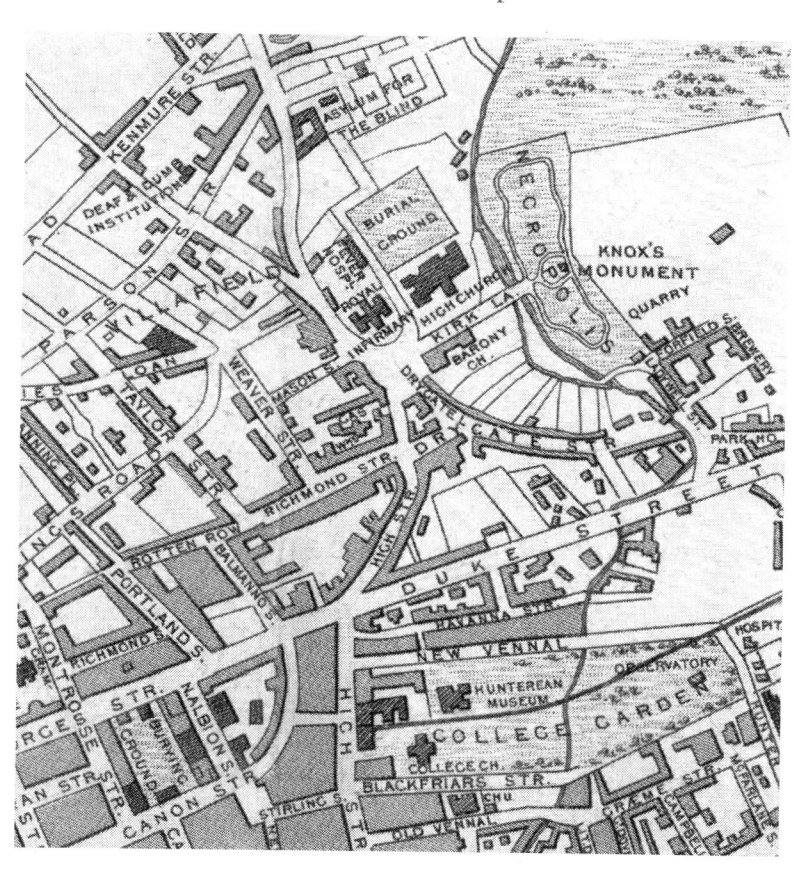

Extended Adam Block, new Fever Block and Glasgow University (College) in High Street by J Rapkin 1854[11]

39

Early Hospital Organisation

In 1830, there were six main Committees of Management of GRI and senior members of staff were co-opted onto more than one committee. Some committees were formed when required, such as a 'fever committee'.

Committees of Management for Glasgow Royal Infirmary, 1831[7]

Dr **Moses Steven Buchanan**[7] was a physician at GRI, who wrote the history of the first 30 years of the Institution. This archive survived and has provided us with valuable early information regarding the management of the enterprise and reveals the recurrent difficulties. Since most individuals on the main subcommittee were unpaid, it was crucial to co-opt those who would contribute and not those simply looking for prestige. There were 27 Directors that included the Professors of Anatomy and Medicine of the University, the President of the FPSG, the Lord

Moses Buchanan[5]

Provost of Glasgow and Dean of Guild. Eight Directors were appointed after nomination and ballot from public bodies and 10 were also elected by ballot for the Main Subcommittee of GRI, the 'General Court of Subscribers', from subscribers and work contributors. It is not clear how many were on this latter committee but it appeared to have control and the final say in any change of policy suggested by the Directors. Clearly, those who 'paid the piper', did actually 'call the tune'.

The **House Committee** is likely to have been involved in the major decisions relating to the planning for improvements and additions to the GRI estate. The **Subscriptions Committee** of 9 individuals dealt with all matters of income and this was arguably the most crucial of all the management groups to the survival of the Institution. The **Accounts Committee** of 5 members was likely charged with all matters relating to yearly income and expenditure and would be led by the GRI accountant. The **Weekly Committee** of 5 changed monthly, with each member serving for 3 months each year, and dealing with matters relating to the GRI's relationship with the outside world. In particular, they would probably have dealt with complaints made by visitors, medical or surgical attendants or students. The **Medical Committee** of 6 probably dealt with matters medical and surgical and this almost certainly included apothecary stock of medicaments, leeches and equipment. Leeches were a substantial expenditure for the Infirmary and in 1829, they cost £89, all 22,400 of them. Castor oil on the other hand cost much less. Finally, the **Provisions Committee** of 13 ensured that the GRI kitchen had sufficient food, wine, victuals and fuel. The tasks of this committee were often made easier by the gifting in kind of supplies of bread, food and fuel by suppliers in Glasgow. For example, 150 tons of coal was apparently gifted annually for heating purposes.

By the 1850s, the demands upon the Infirmary were increasing almost exponentially due, in part, to an increasing confidence in the Institution by the people of Glasgow and in part to the rapid increase in the population within the City. It was also becoming clear from experience gleaned by other comparable hospitals that medical and surgical cases should be separated to prevent spread of infection and so plans were laid for a new Surgical Block. The decision was made to employ the architects **Clarke** and **Bell** in the rather novel design that was an early example of the pavilion plan with two ward wings placed in line on either side of a central block containing the main staircase.

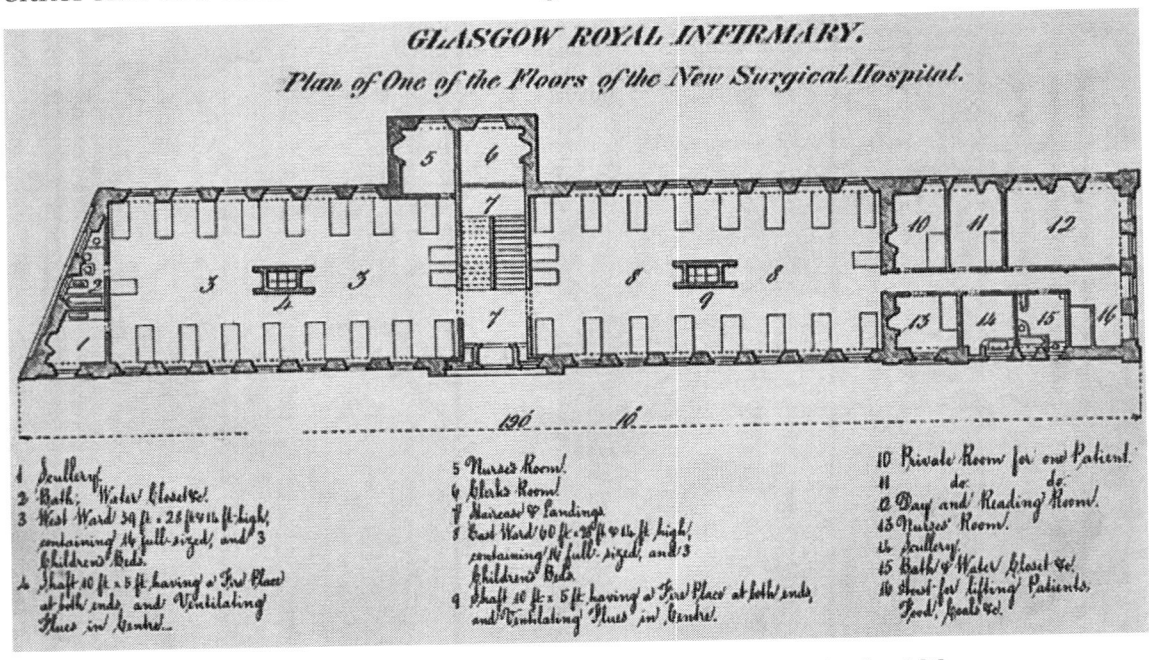

Floor Plan for a floor of the new Surgical Block[8]

Nurse's rooms, sculleries, side rooms, bathrooms, water closets and a hoist for patients were placed at the end of the wards. A new up-to-date operating theatre was constructed centrally in the upper floor, horseshoe in shape to accommodate up to 200 students. Two open fires were placed back to back in the centre of the ward, for heating. The new design also innovated with a day room on each floor for convalescent patients for the first time. There were pleasure grounds for ambulant cases to the North laid out in 3 terraces

Adam Block, Fever Hospital and new Surgical Block, 1861[5]

Glasgow Royal Infirmary: Original Fever and Surgical Blocks from Courtyard, 1880[9]

with a veranda for shade and shelter. This new build brought the total bed complement of GRI to over 600. It's opening in 1861 completed the original Infirmary surrounding a courtyard on three sides and cost £12,206. By 1886, by agreement with the City Council and for reasons of public health, infectious fevers were excluded from GRI. Patients were thereafter hospitalised in the new Glasgow Corporation Fever Hospital at Belvidere. Around this time, although physicians at GRI had probably started to use the very helpful monaural 'stethoscope' invented by **René T H Laennec** in

Glasgow Royal Infirmary – The Auld Hoose (Adam) with Vicar's Alley on the right[3]

1816, they still relied heavily upon accurate observation and skill for diagnosis. As part of the free outpatient service to the community at large, one of the surgeons attended the 'Waiting Room' daily giving advice to both medical and surgical cases. It was hoped, apparently, that each patient would see the same doctor at subsequent visits and that there would be 'recorded facts' as to the condition and to the means of cure. A Dispensary pupil made up prescriptions for attendees to the waiting room. It is not clear where this waiting room was. Most likely, it would have been in one of the smaller buildings on the West side of the courtyard with the laundry and nurses sleeping quarters and possibly even where the Admission Block and Dispensary would be built in 1909. This Block would eventually be transformed into the Casualty Department and would be used until the 1980s when the new Accident and Emergency Department opened in the Phase 3 Queen Elizabeth building on Alexandra Parade.

Original Adam Block of Glasgow Royal Infirmary and Cathedral from Castle Street, 1880[9]

References

[1]. Reproduced with the permission of the National Library of Scotland
http://www.maps.nls.uk/index.html

[2]. Image courtesy of Craig Richardson and the Medical Illustration Department at Glasgow Royal Infirmary.

[3]. Images courtesy of Andrew McAinsh and the Royal College of Physicians of Glasgow archive, 2018.

[4]. A Medical History of Scotland. John D Comrie, 2nd edition. Published by the Wellcome Historical Medical Museum, 1932.
http://www.electricscotland.com/history/medical/scottishmedicine02.pdf

[5]. Images courtesy of Alistair Tough, Archive Department, Mitchell Library, Glasgow, 2018.

[6]. A Short History of Glasgow Royal Infirmary. John Patrick, 1940. Written for Colvilles magazine, Messrs Colvilles Ltd, Steel Manufacturer – Courtesy of Mr Alistair Tough, Archive Department, Mitchell Library, Glasgow.

[7]. History of the Glasgow Royal Infirmary. Dr Moses Steven Buchanan, Glasgow, 1832. – Courtesy of Mr Alistair Tough, Archive Department, Mitchell Library, Glasgow.

[8]. Historic Hospitals and their architecture.
https://historic-hospitals.com/2018/10/26/the-first-glasgow-royal-infirmary/

[9]. Image courtesy of the Welcome Medical Library archive.

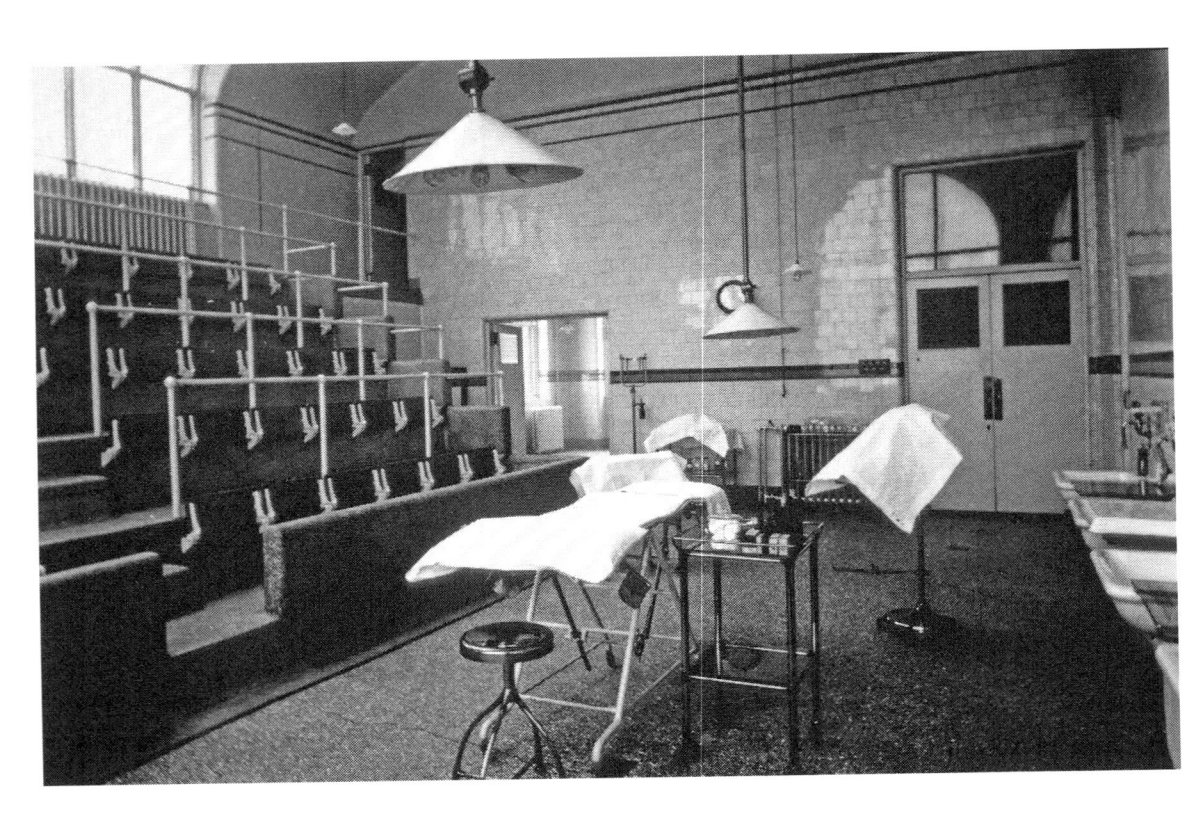

Teaching Theatre of the Lister Surgical Block, GRI[1]

Chapter 4

Twin Scourges of Surgery

The latter half of the 19th Century was a significant era for surgery and Scotland was in the vanguard. Step by step, pioneers from Glasgow Royal Infirmary changed the scope and safety of invasive surgery forever by methods for infection control initially then later for infection elimination. This radically improved the patient's experience of the procedures and their survival from them. Before that work had started, the safe rendering of the patient unconscious in a controlled fashion solved the nightmare of consciousness during painful surgery.

Anaesthesia from Edinburgh

It all started in Harvard Medical School when **William Thomas Green Morton** attended the chemistry lectures of Dr **Charles T Jackson** and was shown the anaesthetic properties of ether. Morton did not graduate but became a dentist and on Sept 30th 1846, performed a painless tooth extraction after administration of ether to the patient. Shortly thereafter, Boston surgeon **Henry Jacob Bigelow** painlessly removed a tumour from the neck of a patient at the Massachusetts General Hospital. When news of the trials of sulphuric ether by Dr Morton had reached him from Boston in 1846, the Professor of Medicine and Midwifery in Edinburgh, Sir **James Young Simpson** began his experiments with the

James Young Simpson[2]

anaesthetic properties of ether. **Richard Formby**, a Liverpool physician, drew his attention to chloric ether (impure Chloroform). Dr **David Waldie**, a Scottish doctor turned chemist working in Liverpool, managed to purify it and may have supplied Simpson with a small volume of the pure chloroform for his experiments. Ether and impure chloroform had been used in Veterinary Medicine for 5 years but up till then had been considered too toxic for use in humans. In early 1847, Simpson was the first to show, despite opposition, how the safe use of sulphuric ether could revolutionise childbirth. In November 1847, he experimented next with chloroform that was delivered by the drop method (i.e. upon lint wound round a mask). He discovered its superior effect and thereby provided a platform for its use during all surgical procedures. Chloroform was rapidly and enthusiastically adopted at GRI one week after Simpson's announcement. Later, the possible complications of epiglottal obstruction and the rare complication of sudden death were recognised. More certain in effect and simpler to administer, chloroform rapidly became the anaesthetic of choice in Scotland. Usually, the resident doctor administered the agent despite warnings that experience was preferable. Queen Victoria apparently was given chloroform during the birth of Prince Leopold in 1853.

Rise of Antisepsis

Up to the mid-19th Century, however, anaesthesia was not the main problem in surgery. It didn't matter who performed the operation, how skilful he was with the knife, how rapidly the operation was concluded or how sharp the instruments were. The dreadful scourge of surgery of any type was post-operative sepsis.[3][4] Hospital gangrene, erysipelas, septicaemia and pyaemia were almost regarded as inevitable and were so prevalent that infection was called the 'hospital disease'. Presumably, one had a better chance of recovery if surgery was performed at home and indeed many minor operations were performed by choice in this environment by those who could afford it. It was hoped and probably assumed by managers and surgeons alike that moving to the brand new hospital building in 1861 with up-to-date theatres and wards would reduce the incidence of this ghastly and potentially fatal condition. Unfortunately, they were all to be disappointed. Suppuration and 'laudable' pus with its associated stench continued to be the norm. Change came in the figure of Joseph **Lister,** later Baron Lister. He had trained in London and then in 1854, had spent time as an assistant surgeon and lecturer in Edinburgh with Professor **James Syme,** a pioneering Scottish surgeon. In 1861, Lister was appointed to the Regius Chair of Surgery of the University of Glasgow at GRI on the death of Prof **James Adair Laurie** and was forced to spent 15 months in teaching and research since there were no wards available in GRI for his use at that time.[6]

Joseph Lister[1]

Old Glasgow College, High Street[5]

His teaching classroom was situated in the inner quadrangle of the Old College of the University of Glasgow on High Street where he also spent time profitably investigating the clotting of blood. When Lister started ward duties in 1862 as an experienced surgeon, he was given ward 24, male, with 14 beds and ward 25, female, with 21 beds. He was a popular teacher with students and his class in systematic surgery numbered 182 in his first year at GRI. Lister's initial interest was in limb amputation and he duly reported that between 1862 and 1865, 45 to 50% of all his amputation cases died of post-operative sepsis despite all his efforts and the efforts of junior staff and nurses. During that period, it was the norm to find epidemics of septic infection among the surgical cases in the surgical wards. At intervals, surgical wards at GRI had to be closed for cleaning and disinfection when this occurred. Wards in general were not well equipped with washing facilities and instruments employed during surgery or for dressing wounds were used over and over again. Operating coats were worn both outside and in theatre and surgical ligatures to be used in theatre were carried in buttonholes. Clearly, surgeons of the age had been unaware of the Treatise on Puerperal Fever[7] by Dr **Alexander Gordon** (1752-1799) of Aberdeen where in 1795, he recognised the contagious features of puerperal fever and its transmission by medical attendants or nurses who had been exposed to the disease.

Around this time, a new instrument appeared to assist diagnosis of infection so prevalent after surgery. Following publication of both 'A Manual of Medical Thermometry' by the German Physician, **Carl R A Wunderlich**, and 'Medical Thermometry' by **Clifford Allbutt**, an English Physician, the clinical thermometer would have come into use at GRI in the mid 1870s. Albutt's version was about 6 inches in length and had a constriction above the bulb that soon became the standard model.

In 1866, the 51st Annual Report commented upon the 'Dispensary' providing free medical care for poor citizens who could not afford the cost of medical advice. Lister did not attend the Dispensary, being an academic, but he would have approved of the decision to ensure that two physicians and two surgeons of not less than six years standing would carry out its duties. The provision of such free advice from experienced staff for the surrounding population was one of the main reasons for the esteem that GRI was held in by that population. It also ensured their support financially through difficult times.

In 1865, Dr **Thomas Anderson**, Professor of Chemistry at the University of Glasgow, drew Lister's attention to the work of **Louis Pasteur** suggesting that micro-organisms, minute forms of life, were the cause of the putrefaction, and not emanations from the air. Antiseptics such as tincture of iodine and derivatives of coal tar had been already tried and found unsatisfactory. Indeed Dr **Jules Lemaire** in Paris had written a book on the use of the antiseptic properties of carbolic acid in preventing wound infection during surgery in 1863. His methods never caught on outside the French Capital and Lemaire appeared to be using a much more dilute solution than Lister. Professor Lister heard almost incidentally that carbolic acid treatment of sewage at Carlyle had reduced the stench and unpleasantness of the Treatment Works. Anderson provided Lister with crude carbolic acid for his initial experiments and then when a purer form of the chemical became available, Lister trialled the application of a formula of diluted carbolic acid to his instruments, hands, wounds, bandages and experimented with antisepsis in all aspects of his surgical work. He particularly used the carbolic solution in compound fractures where infection was guaranteed. Lister was fastidious in all attempts to exclude bacteria from the wounds and clearly had better outcomes than Lemaire.

Lister's male surgical ward 24 with a student dresser in short white jacket[2]

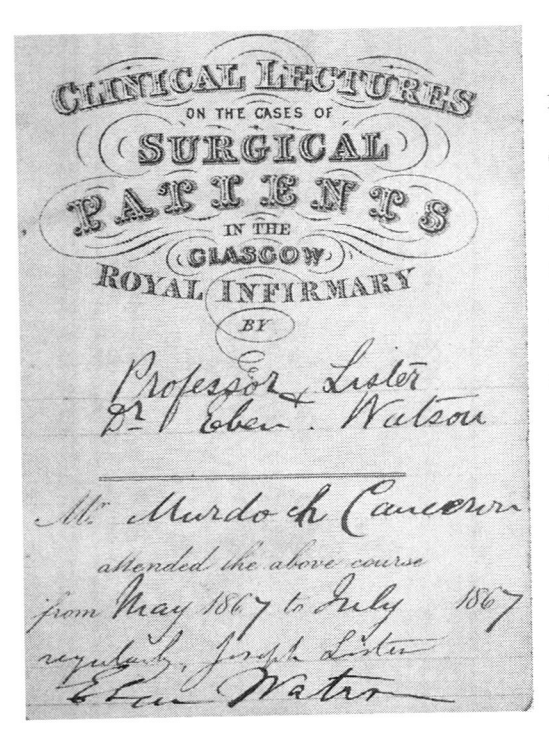

Lister's Surgical Course Certificate for Murdoch Cameron[8]

Professor Lister published initial results in 1867 justifying his reasoning and citing his falling death rate. He also tried to reduce bacteria in the air of his theatre by using a carbolic spray. This spray went through several iterations and ended up a steam aerosol. A local instrument maker, Mr **Andrew Brown** of George Street made several types of spray for this research. Lister then reported that the overall use of antisepsis in his male accident ward, ward 24, between 1865 and 1869 had reduced his surgical mortality from 50% to 15%. Some British surgeons began to visit GRI to find out how to use dilute carbolic in theatre and on dressings. His pupils and trainee surgeons would also pass on his principles and methods. One of these gifted trainees, **William Macewen**, would change the model of antisepsis into one of asepsis and thereby herald in a new age for surgery largely free of postoperative infection. Another trainee, **Murdoch Cameron** would change the practice of obstetrics by the development of the caesarean section in 1888 at the Glasgow Maternity Hospital.

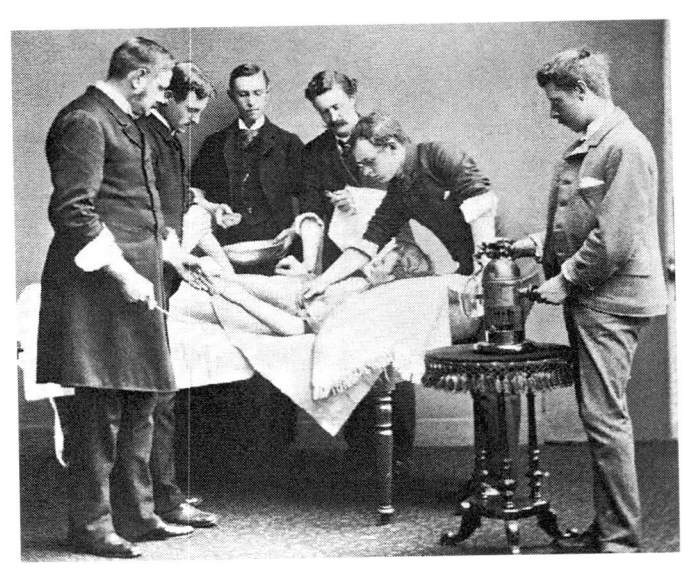

Victorian surgeons use carbolic spray for antisepsis around 1871[9]

Lister also experimented with ligatures for arterial bleeding and found that carbolic-sterilised silk prevented suppuration following surgery. Irritation did result from the presence of silk as a foreign body however, so he embarked upon experiments with sterile absorbable catgut. This was successful in elimination of both infection and irritation. Like **Ignaz Semmelweis** before him, however, his research, claims of originality, and methods of antisepsis were rejected for a time by some GRI and UK surgeons though were more rapidly adopted worldwide, particularly in the USA. Most surgeons in England apparently baulked at the rigmarole, and the supposed waste of time, money and energy. Lister was promoted to Professor of Surgery in Edinburgh University in 1869 and continued his research into the prevention of wound infection with antisepsis. It was only really when he followed Sir **William Ferguson** as Professor of Clinical Surgery at King's College, London in the late 1870s that his methods gained credence across the United Kingdom. He eventually met Pasteur in person in 1878 at a meeting in Paris. Lister had managed to completely change the global surgical approach to the prevention of wound sepsis and had introduced antiseptic surgery to the world. By his example, he had set the scene for his young pupil at GRI, Macewen, to bring modern aseptic surgery into the 20th Century and to remove the fear associated with 'hospitals'.[6]

Professor Joseph Lister, OM. PC. PRS. London[10]

Lister is also known for his early research on the coagulation of blood and he was clearly influenced by the work of Andrew Buchanan, one of his predecessors at GRI. He probably was the first to demonstrate scientifically that there were two systems operative in blood coagulation, the intrinsic and the extrinsic. Lister also published on chloroform anaesthesia advocating use of the conjunctival reflex for assessment of the level of anaesthesia and advising fasting before surgery. Since he believed that experience was not required for the use of chloroform, surgeons at GRI controlled the teaching and administration of anaesthesia for several decades thereafter. Lister was President of the Royal

Society (1885-1900) and President of the British Association (1896). He had many honours, British and foreign and was made a Baron in 1897.

Lister died in 1912.[11]

Aseptic Surgery Triumphs

Professor Sir **William Macewen, C.B, LL.D, DSc**, graduated from the University of Glasgow in 1869. He was a pupil of Professor Lister's in the Department of Surgery at GRI and dresser in his wards as a student rising to become an assistant surgeon at GRI in 1875. He became a surgeon 2 years later aged 29 with wards, then a lecturer in systematic surgery at GRI School of Medicine.[6] Early after qualification, he had spent time as Superintendent of the new City Fever Hospital at Belvidere. While there, he revealed his engineering flair and genius by experimenting with rubberised elastic catheters inserted via the mouth into the trachea in cases of laryngeal obstruction due to diphtheria. This was the first endotracheal tube and was an alternative to tracheotomy. His innovation to preserve life in respiratory obstruction was soon to be crucial in the new speciality of anaesthetics. Macewen fully supported his mentor's antiseptic principles but gradually expanded upon the principle and introduced the complete aseptic theatre environment by adopting the scrubbing of hands/arms for cleaning of skin and disinfection, and by steam sterilisation of surgical instruments. He also introduced sterile surgical gowns, dressings and swabs. Finally he fully adopted the new chloroform anaesthesia to reduce the horror of surgical induced pain. He was one of the first to ask his colleagues administering the anaesthetic to use the endotracheal anaesthesia with equipment that he had

William Macewen[1]

personally designed and developed. Macewen introduced catgut hardened in chromic acid that not only sterilised it but also lengthened the time for its absorption and he published this work in 1881.

Macewen was one of the most creative and innovative surgeons of his era. His first major research was the pathophysiology of bone and bone growth in a city where rickets was endemic. Macewen's new operation for genu valgum – linear osteotomy – was a major advance in technique that was published in 1880. He even ensured that his chisels had the proper temper and toughness for the task and, to ensure sterility, had eliminated the practice of using wooden handles that make them more difficult to sterilise. This work was outstanding and was accomplished long before radiological guidance was introduced into GRI at the end of the Century. In 1886, he published a new and effective treatment for inguinal hernia that so far had eluded surgeons. In 1888, Macewen addressed the British Medical Association Congress in Glasgow and described his pioneering surgery for cerebral tumours or infection. This presentation propelled Macewen's recognition in surgery worldwide. He was at a meeting in Berlin two years later where Curt **Schimmelbusch** demonstrated his apparatus for sterilising dressings and instruments with steam. This became the forerunner of the autoclave and was adopted quickly by Macewen at GRI.

Sir William Macewen FRS[1]

In 1892 he left GRI with his appointment as Regius Professor of Surgery at the Western Infirmary Glasgow (WIG) on the death of Professor Sir **George H B McLeod**. Macewen had never really been involved in teaching large numbers of students but developed a novel surgical laboratory at the WIG and became a popular, successful and inspiring teacher. While there, he described his own revolutionary approach to the problem of chronic middle ear infection and its

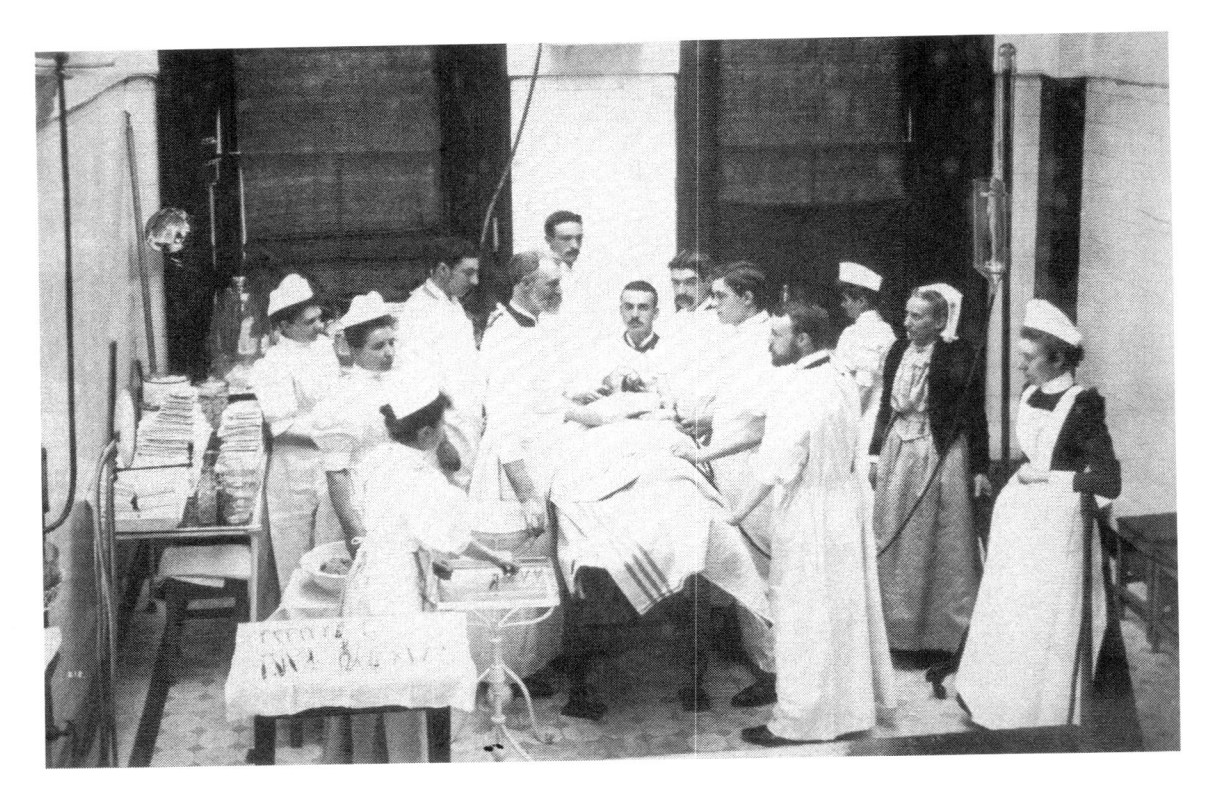

Sir William Macewen operating in 1892 with an anaesthetist sitting and Matron, Rebecca Strong, second from the right[1]

surgical treatment. He defined the clear indications for successful mastoid surgery. It was also at the WIG that he pioneered thoracic surgery with considerable success. He taught that, after surgery, wound dressings should be left for 2 weeks if there were no signs of infection, that unnecessary intraoperative damage to tissue should be avoided and that there should be minimal use of antiseptics. He also emphasised the importance of absorbable sutures. These steps transformed the recovery times and significantly reduced the mortality of his patients.

Macewen wisely introduced anaesthesia training to the student curriculum much in the way that vaccination training was compulsory. He required well trained nursing staff for his

Sir William Macewen FRS. by Charles R Dowell[8]

pioneering advances in surgery, particularly surgery of the brain, and favoured a systematic basic training for nurses leading to advanced training and fully supported GRI Matron Rebecca Strong in all her endeavours to make nursing a profession and improve standards at GRI. Concern was being raised in 1882 at the number of deaths thought to relate to chloroform anaesthesia and so he eventually supported the formalisation of training to make anaesthetics a post-graduate speciality. Deaths may have been related to either obstruction of the airway by the tongue or a sensitisation of the heart to adrenaline that led to ventricular fibrillation and circulatory arrest. Despite these significant advances in understanding, however, it was 1905 before the first anaesthetist, Dr **Laurie Watson**, was appointed at GRI as a specialist on a salary of £25 per annum. The second, Dr **H Prescott Fairlie** was 4 years later.[12]

Erskine House, Site of Scottish Hospital for Limbless[13]

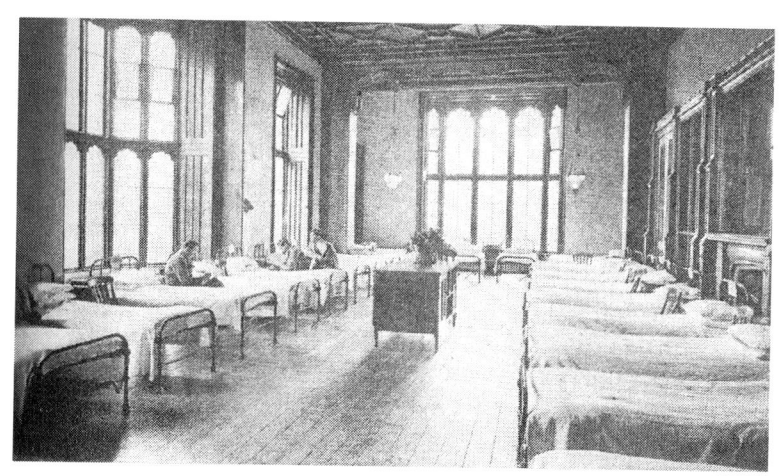

Erskine Hospital Dormitory[13]

Among his many honours, Macewen was knighted in 1902. He continued to be active, however, and at the beginning of the war, he was consultant surgeon to Naval Forces in Scotland. Despite this extra work and in his 6th decade around 1914/15, he realised that Scottish soldier amputees from the trenches could only have limbs fitted at Roehampton, London. He immediately determined that Scotland needed its own facility to provide for its wounded men. Macewen became the driving force behind the acquisition of Erskine House, loaned initially by **Thomson Aikman** then later purchased for the hospital by Sir **Robert Reid** for the value of the agricultural land only. The House was given gratis. After an

Erskine Hospital Lounge and Recreation Hall[13]

appeal, £100,000 was collected representing £8M in modern currency. He personally became involved in the building of the Princess Louise Scottish Hospital for Limbless Sailors and Soldiers[13] that accepted its first casualty in October 1916. Macewen became involved in all aspects of the design and manufacture of limbs in willow wood that was chosen by him. He designed the 'Erskine Limb', and manufactured them using the skills of Clydeside shipbuilders and patients themselves for production. By 1920, almost 10,000 artificial limbs had been made and fitted in the hospital's workshops. Macewen worked for 47 years as a practising surgeon at GRI and WIG. Extraordinarily productive, he was an innovative individualist, and a brilliant visionary in diverse areas of surgery, which put him ahead of his time. Undeniably a genius at his craft, he managed to bring surgery at GRI into the 20th Century single handedly before any other group or any other hospital worldwide. Not only that, by supporting Mrs Rebecca Strong, Macewen helped to propel GRI nursing and nurse training into the first division that became even more important as the surgical specialities emerged.

Macewen died in 1924.[14]

References

[1]. Images courtesy of Alistair Tough, Archive Department, Mitchell Library, Glasgow

[2]. Image courtesy of the Welcome Medical Library archive

[3]. The Healers: A History of Medicine in Scotland. David Hamilton. 1981

[4]. A Medical History of Scotland. John D Comrie, 2nd edition. Published by the Wellcome Historical Medical Museum, 1932.
http://www.electricscotland.com/history/medical/scottishmedicine02.pdf

[5]. Image of the old College
https://canmore.org.uk/site/44095/glasgow-high-street-old-college

[6]. The Royal: The History of Glasgow Royal Infirmary 1794 – 1994. Jacqueline Jenkinson, Michael Moss and Iain Russell. 1994

[7]. Dr Alexander Gordon (1752-1799) and Contagious Puerperal Fever. Peter M Dunn. 1795.
http://fn.bmj.com/content/78/3/F232

[8]. Images courtesy of Andrew McAinsh and the Royal College of Physicians of Glasgow archive, 2018.

[9]. Image courtesy of Mr Whelan, Caedmon College, Whitby
https://www.pinterest.co.uk/mrwhelan_ccw/surgery-and-anatomy/?eq=Surgery%20and%20anatomy&etslf=18912

[10]. Image Courtesy of the National Portrait Gallery

[11]. Professor Joseph Lister obituary, Royal College of Surgeons.
https://livesonline.rcseng.ac.uk/client/en_GB/lives/search/detailnonmodal/ent:$0 02f$002fSD_ASSET$002f0$002f334967/onequ=%22rcs%3A+E000500%22&rt=false %7C%7C%7CIDENTIFIER%7C%7C%7CResource+Identifier

[12]. Early Glasgow Anaesthesia. Dr Betty Bradford. Proceedings of the History of Anaesthesia Society, June 1995, Glasgow.
http://www.histansoc.org.uk/uploads/9/5/5/2/9552670/volume_17.pdf

[13]. Professor K R Paterson, from a talk given to the Senior Fellows at the Royal College of Physicians and Surgeons of Glasgow on 7th November, 2018.

[14]. Obituary for Sir William Macewen. British Medical Journal, March 29, 1924, 603-608.

Adam Block (The Auld Hoose), from Castle Street, 1880[1]

Chapter 5

St Mungo's Medical College

Throughout the mid-19th Century, Glasgow Royal Infirmary remained solvent from day-to-day through a combination of personal and family subscriptions with contributions from factories, mills, collieries, foundries and commercial enterprises. This was augmented by generous personal giving from those with means and through Parish and Kirk contributions. The collection of funds for the Infirmary became a specialist activity for the treasurer who was usually an accountant. By this time, the financial needs of GRI were virtually insatiable and new ways were constantly required to raise money for this community endeavour 'par excellance'. The donations and legacies from the most wealthy benefactors and philanthropists were particularly beneficial for any capital projects to improve the GRI estate and crucial for the new building work contemplated at the end of the Century.

Small improvements to the service continued after the building of the Lister Surgical Block and were made during the Victorian era which was relatively prosperous for Glasgow. In 1871, a larger dispensary for outpatients was opened and 2 years later, the number of attending physicians and surgeons was increased to 5 of each speciality to cope with the workload. In 1875, a hoist was fitted to surgical house to facilitate movement of sick and injured patients and in 1878, improvements in the hygiene of patients resulted when baths were fitted to all wards of the Infirmary. In 1882, the telephone was introduced throughout the hospital that permitted ward staff to talk to seniors in their homes and all board and lodging paid by resident doctors was stopped. In the same decade, lighting in wards and theatres in GRI was electrified.

By 1870, the original GRI had managed to build a new surgical block, maintain the building estate and provide up-to-date charitable care not only for the working poor but also the destitute and infirm of the area. An increasingly open door policy enabled medical students to see as much of medicine and surgery as possible and attend clinical lectures delivered in the wards by physicians. In fact, GRI trained all future generations of physicians and surgeons from the University of Glasgow until the opening of the **Western Infirmary (WIG)** in 1874, which was also a voluntary hospital. Although the scourges of typhus, smallpox and typhoid had disappeared with the advances in public health and vaccination, tuberculosis remained ever present in the adult population and whooping cough and measles killed or maimed vast numbers of children.

Medical Student Training

From as early as 1845, the University of Glasgow Court had found the Old College buildings off High Street in the centre of the city inadequate for teaching and research and realised that a move to rebuild in the West end of the City was inevitable. A timely plan to sell off the High Street site to a railway company failed at that time but in 1864, the Old College site was indeed sold to the City of Glasgow Union Railway. The University of Glasgow then rebuilt at Gilmorehill which was West of the City centre. GRI was too remote for students to have clinical teaching so a new Western 'University' Hospital was designed by **John Burnet** and opened in 1874. By that time as the students of Glasgow University left GRI for the new Western Infirmary hospital to complete the clinical aspects of their training, the Professor of Medicine, **William Tennant Gairdner**, had been a physician at GRI for 12 years. He and the Professor of Surgery, **George H B MacLeod**, needed to transfer their professorial chairs from GRI to the new University hospital in the West of the city. Gairdner was a philosopher and well-loved teacher who directed young minds along scientific paths in medicine. Science was becoming important to doctors as crucial discoveries were made about the pathogenesis of infection and the effects of chloroform. If truth be told, he appears to have been delighted by the move to the new hospital. He suddenly found himself unencumbered by the egos of established hospital physicians and was therefore able to improve the structure of, and approach to, the clinical training of his medical students. Apparently, clinical tuition at GRI had, up till then, been somewhat 'ad hoc' with little co-operation between Units. Many of the senior academic staff felt that the training resources of the GRI were not being used wisely. They were unable to influence or change the culture because of the autonomy of hospital consultants and the long-standing weakness of University influence at ground level in GRI.

With the transfer of the University students to Gilmorehill and clinical studies being undertaken at the WIG, GRI was now short of the medical student numbers required to become dressers in the surgical units, locums on the medical wards and house officers in the medical and surgical units. Given the existential nature of this problem for a teaching hospital, the Board of GRI decided to develop their own Medical School on the model of the long established London Teaching Hospitals. A supplementary Charter was obtained that gave the Board power to provide facilities and accommodation for teaching in medicine and in surgery. Classrooms were found within the GRI estate, and lecturers appointed to develop and facilitate the creation of an in-house, **Royal Infirmary, School of Medicine.** The Board were careful to align the School with the larger **Anderson College of Medicine** close by in College Street off High Street. The two Medical Schools could share both pre and post-clinical lectures and facilities.[2][3] Glasgow Royal Infirmary School of Medicine was in the vanguard of Institutions removing any restriction on women registering for training as doctors by it's compliance with the 1876 Enabling Act of Parliament. This permitted British medical authorities to license all qualified applicants whatever their gender. Other schools included King's and Queen's College of Ireland in Dublin and the Royal Free Hospital, London. GRI admitted the first two female students in 1884 who were permitted to attend all clinical classes, all pathological demonstrations and to become house physicians and surgeons. These women, **Janet Hunter** of Ayr and **Sarah Gray** of London, both passed the Triple Examination in 1888 and were

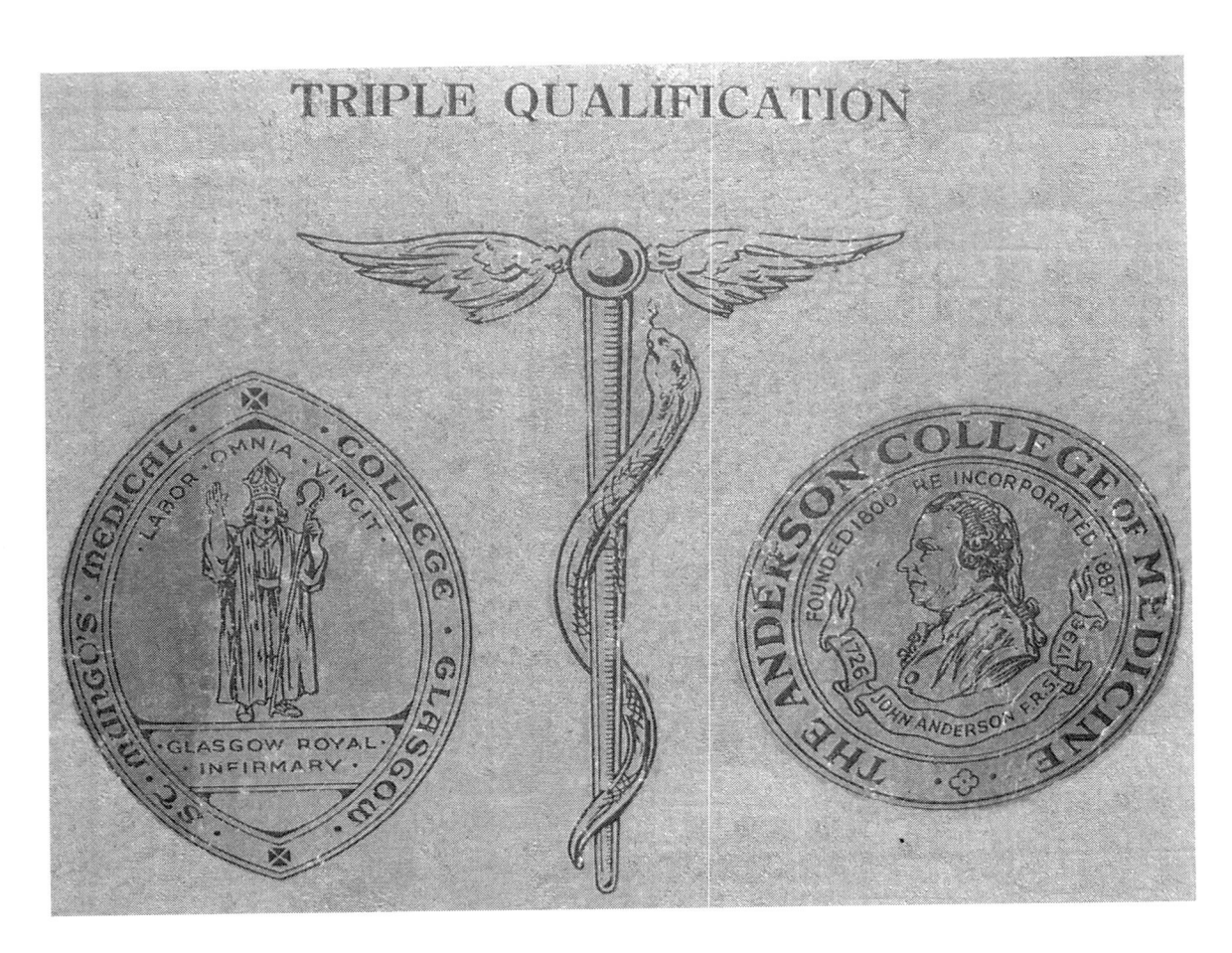

The Two Triple Qualification Colleges in Glasgow[5]

licensed as doctors. From 1886, students from GRI and Anderson's Colleges graduated in medicine by the '**Triple Qualification**'[6] in medicine, surgery and midwifery. They were Licentiates of the Royal College of Physicians and Surgeons of Glasgow, the Royal College of Physicians of Edinburgh and the Royal College of Surgeons of Edinburgh. They could also study for licenses from England or Dublin. Sir William Macewen was unhappy with the compromises in space and facilities for the students who were so very important to the Institution. He managed to persuade the Board to fund, by public donation, a purpose-built

St Mungo's Medical College

St Mungo's College, situated North of the surgical block and South of the Blind Asylum. This up-to-date facility contained a dissecting room, anatomical

64

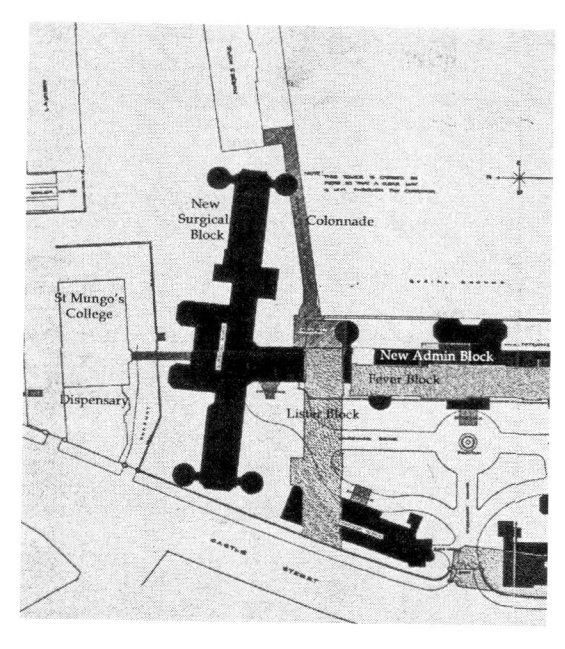

St Mungo's in relation to old and new GRI

museum, osteology and reading room, lecture room for 150, classrooms for chemistry and physiology, a large general medical library and administrative offices. The new College building opened for student training in 1888. Unfortunately, one year before in 1887, the Anderson Medical College had moved to Dumbarton Road closer to the University of Glasgow. This was due to an increasing unsuitability of their cramped central premises that lacked space for laboratories. Anderson's students who previously attended GRI classes therefore began attending the Western Infirmary for clinical instruction because of their proximity to that hospital. GRI now had inadequate numbers of medical students who on qualification would have become house officers. The GRI Board appeared to have enough on their plate at the time so called time on their school and in late 1888, they handed over training of medical students to a brand new incorporated Medical College which had more financial protection in law and easier access to capital.

St Mungo's Medical College [2][3][6] was designed as a complete medical faculty with professors from GRI and Anderson's College. It absorbed the classrooms, laboratories, museum and libraries necessary for a medical course from the GRI Medical School and moved into it's well appointed premises. The Library

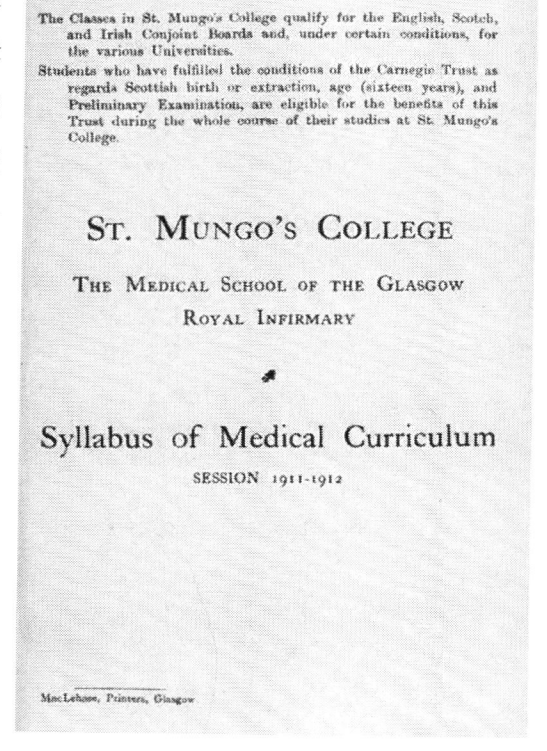

St Mungo's Syllabus[7]

65

became the meeting place for the newly formed GRI Medical Society. A Board of 27 men who were appointed by the Managers of GRI, governed the College.

St Mungo's Medical Class graduating 1937 with Professors. Reference to staff and students[8]

St Mungo's College initially prospered because their fees were lower than the University of Glasgow.[5] It followed the GRI Medical School in complying with the 1876 Enabling Act of Parliament by admitting women students who were permitted to attend all clinical classes, all pathological demonstrations and who could become house physicians and house surgeons. Further, by accepting Jewish applicants, St Mungos's College was a popular choice for many students who came from the

St Mungo's Medal for Biology[4]

St Mungo's Football Team, 1936[9]

USA. At that time in the United States, most individuals of Jewish faith were quietly banned from studying medicine in mainland USA by the operation of less than secret quotas. These individuals could obtain their own American Diplomas by sitting and passing the Triple Examination then passing their own State examination which, when successful, permitted them to practice in mainland USA. While the College had many fewer student clubs than the University with its sizeable student base, St Mungo's mostly male students were known to regularly challenge other medical schools to football. The photograph represents the St Mungo's football in team in 1936 playing against the Aberdeen Medical students with many of these individuals graduating in the Triple Examination of 1937.

Despite incorporation, financial pressures on the St Mungo's College Governors who ran the medical school continued. While a University education was more prestigious, most individuals of modest means would have chosen St Mungo's and GRI because of cost. However, in 1901, Carnegie Trust grants to pay class fees at University became available for less well-off medical students and so a University degree became possible for this group. At the same time, the supply of medical students at GRI from England, Ireland and Wales began to dry up with the opening of new Medical Schools in the provincial cities of England. It was an existential problem for St Mungo's College, a staffing issue for *GRI* that required young doctors for locum and house-officer posts and a waste of superb medical and surgical teaching facilities. The struggle with inadequate student numbers at GRI continued and resulted in a request to the GRI Board for financial assistance in 1905. When this was rejected, the Governors attempted to persuade the University of Glasgow to make them an extramural school of the University but this too was unsuccessful. The situation looked bleak financially for St Mungo's College but the University of Glasgow came to the rescue. Circumstances at Gilmorehill Campus had begun to conspire in GRI's favour.

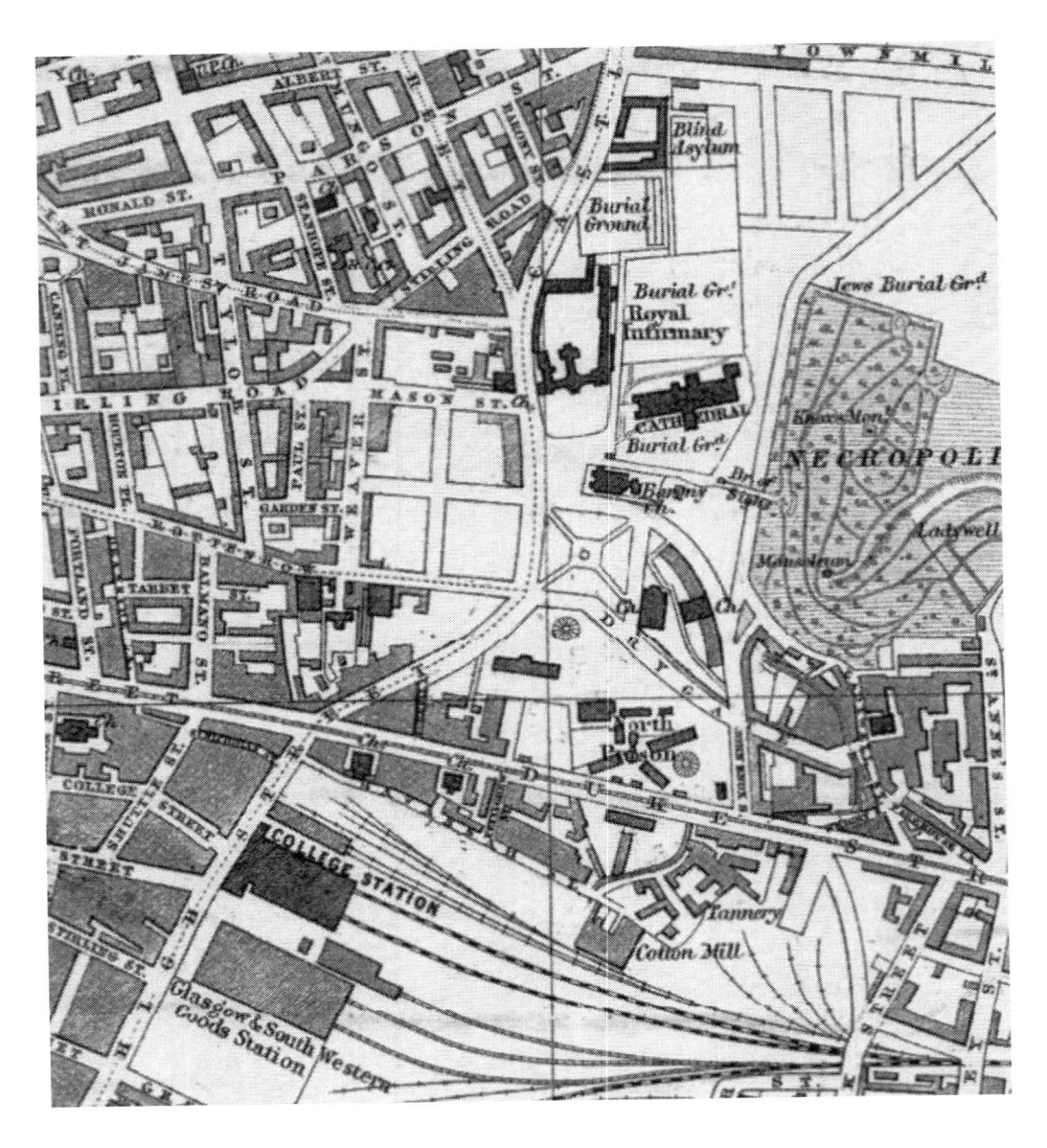

Fully Developed 'old' GRI. College Station has replaced the University of Glasgow. Map by John Bartholomew, 1882[10]

Rapprochement between College and University

Sir Donald MacAlister, the University Principal was an insightful man and a realist. Despite the past difficulties between the University and GRI, he was keen to bring GRI back into the teaching fold. He had become aware that the increasing clinical class sizes at the WIG was beginning to threaten the quality of student teaching. MacAlister introduced GRI to the Trust of the late Dr **Thomas Muirhead** since it was the deceased wish that two clinical Professorships were created in a clinical establishment, site unspecified. The Trust had already turned down a proposal from another Glasgow hospital and was keen to progress the legacy. Four conditions were stipulated by the Trust. Firstly, that the name Muirhead would be associated with each Professorship. Secondly, that the medical establishment would have links to the University. Thirdly, that the establishment would match the £40,000 endowment of the Trust. And finally, that all teaching would be open to women. The agreement between GRI, St Mungo's College and the Muirhead Trust led to a most welcome rapprochement between the University of Glasgow and GRI.

The Muirhead Trust agreed to endow St Mungo's College with a University Muirhead Chair in Medicine and one in Obstetrics. In 1911, after tying up loose ends, the Muirhead Chairs of Medicine and Obstetrics and Gynaecology were filled at GRI as were the St Mungo Chair of Surgery and the St Mungo-Notman Chair of Pathology both funded by The College. The College also continued their policy that medical teaching was open to women on equal terms with men, another key stipulation of the Trust. The clinicians at GRI were now training both the College students and those on the MB course in clinical medicine and surgery although evidence suggests that the University Professors only taught the students of the MB course. After 37 years separated from the University MB students, GRI had returned to its rightful role as the major teaching hospital in Glasgow.

The first Muirhead Professor of Medicine at GRI was **Walter King Hunter** in 1911. He graduated with a BSc in 1888 and MB 2 years later. After postgraduate study in neurology in London and Paris, his MD in 1897 entitled 'The Aetiology of Beriberi' received commendation. He went on to receive a DSc from the University in 1901. While passionate about neurology, Hunter also published on haematology while he was on the junior visiting staff of the Royal Hospital for Sick Children. He quickly became assistant physician at GRI and used his knowledge of the histopathology of the nervous system to study the effects, on the CNS, of venoms of 5 different Indian snakes in collaboration with Captain

Professor Walter K Hunter

George Lamb of the Indian Medical Service. This work was published in the Lancet in 6 instalments between 1904 and 1906. By 1906, he had become physician at GRI and Lecturer in Practice of Medicine to Queen Margaret College of the University of Glasgow which was the University training establishment for women. At this time, he was also consultant physician to the Glasgow Royal Mental Hospital and visiting physician to Bellefield Sanatorium in Lanark. Experience there permitted him to contribute a chapter on 'Treatment' in Maylard's Abdominal Tuberculosis in 1908. After his appointment to the Muirhead Chair, he was recognised as an inspirational bedside teacher of clinical medicine in the mould of Sir William T Gairdner and was known by the nickname 'Uncle Walter' by his housemen and by generations of students. He died in 1947[11] as one of the most distinguished physicians of his generation in Scotland.

The second Muirhead Professor of Medicine at GRI was **Archibald Wilson Harrington**, a graduate of Glasgow in 1900 and MD in 1903. Elected to the junior staff at GRI in 1906, he gained the Fellowship of the Faculty of Physicians and Surgeons of Glasgow (FPSG) in 1912, becoming assistant physician at GRI in 1913. Harrington served in the RAMC in the Balkan theatre with health consequences that continued throughout the remainder of his professional life. Returning to consultant practice at GRI at the war's end, Harrington was appointed lecturer in clinical medicine at the University of Glasgow in 1925. In

Professor Archibald W Harrington

1927, he contributed an excellent teaching chapter 'Examining the Heart' to Finlayson's Clinical Medicine, 1927 edition and with a keen perception of character, appointed **Joseph Houston Wright**[12] to be his personal assistant. Wright could then teach large numbers of students and had access to the University Department of Medicine wards. Joe Wright went on to be an outstanding clinician and cardiologist at GRI, President of the new Royal College of Physicians and Surgeons of Glasgow (RCPSG), and member of the University Court.

Joseph (Joe) H Wright

Harrington was a shy man but nevertheless, worth getting to know in light of his wide knowledge and experience. He always taught by example and his junior staff and students learned quickly. Harrington had an inquisitive mind but, in keeping with the post-war era, did not publish as much as his predecessor. Professor Harrington left office in 1945 and died 1953[13].

The third Muirhead Professor of Medicine at GRI was **Leslie John Davis** who was appointed in 1945 in the newly formed University of Glasgow, Department of Medicine (UDM) at the Royal Infirmary (GRI). It is likely that the Principal **Sir Hector Hetherington** and the Medical Dean **George Wishart** saw in Davis, an opportunity to modernise East Glasgow hospital medicine. He could bring into the hospital, a research programme based on sound scientific and academic principles and introduce laboratory methods into clinical medicine. This would enhance the reputation of the UDM at Glasgow Royal Infirmary for first class clinical practice and teaching. Davis had initially trained as a research medical scientist at the Wellcome Bureau of Scientific Research. Thereafter he was appointed to the staff of the Wellcome Tropical Research Laboratories in Khartoum and practiced

Professor Leslie J Davis

laboratory and clinical medicine there from 1927 to 1930. Davis then became Professor of Pathology at Hong Kong University from 1931 to 1939 but left before the outbreak of hostilities. After a short spell as director of medical laboratories in Bulawayo in Southern Rhodesia, he returned to Edinburgh during the Second World War as an assistant and then lecturer in the Department of Medicine to work in medicine and haematology with **Stanley Davidson (**later **Sir Stanley)**.

The closure of the St Mungo's College Medical School provided Davis with all the accommodation required to set up a laboratory based Department of Medicine adjacent to the Infirmary. The St Mungo's College building had been the base for the St Mungo's Medical School which had opened in 1888 and only closed in 1945 along with the Anderson College on Dumbarton Road following a report from the **Goodenough** Committee which recommended closure of all extra mural medical Colleges. Davis was therefore able to attract young medical graduates to his Unit who had the desire to apply science to clinical practice. Around nuclei of clinical research programs, young researchers were attracted by the buzz and the energy of the Unit and their involvement in clinical teaching. Funding for these young researchers at GRI was usually found from Hall Fellowship, McIntyre or Ure Research Scholarships and were keenly contested. As the first full-time University of Glasgow Professor of Medicine at GRI, Davis began transforming his new department into a teaching and clinical research facility by appointing his senior lecturers strategically.

Professor L J Davis

His senior appointments were **Alex Brown** his deputy, **Edward McGirr, Stuart Douglas, Jim Ferguson** and **Alex McFadzean. Tom McEwan** provided the NHS focus. His juniors included **Arthur Kennedy, Stuart McAlpine, Albert Baikie, Robert Pirie, Robert Hume, Jock Adams, William (Willie) C Watson** and **George P McNicol.**

Despite the lack of a broad clinical experience, Davis forged a centre of excellence in academic medicine at the Royal Infirmary. His strong background in Pathology meant that his own specialty interests lay mainly in Haematology, which was the predominant activity of the UDM during his tenure of the Chair of Medicine. He published work and co-authored a book on megaloblastic anaemias with Alex Brown and worked on nitrogen mustard therapy for lymphoma. Davis regularly published on haemopoietic drugs and treatments and surveyed both the ESR in clinical practice but also the educational value of the classical medical history. He quickly became recognised as a first class clinical haematologist and by his careful choice of appointments, established a reputation for his University clinical unit of excellence in clinical practice and teaching. Davis' laboratory-based department of medicine in the St Mungo's College allowed him to use his experience to mentor his staff on the application of scientific skills to 'clinical practice and research. He gradually helped to transform a mainly clinical hospital into one favourable to laboratory-based research, clinical innovation and sub-specialisation. LJ, as he was known, retired in 1961 aged 60, moved to Yarmouth and, being keen on sailing, signed on with the Royal National Lifeboat Institution to help crew the local lifeboat and continue to serve the community.

Stuart McAlpine

Willie Watson

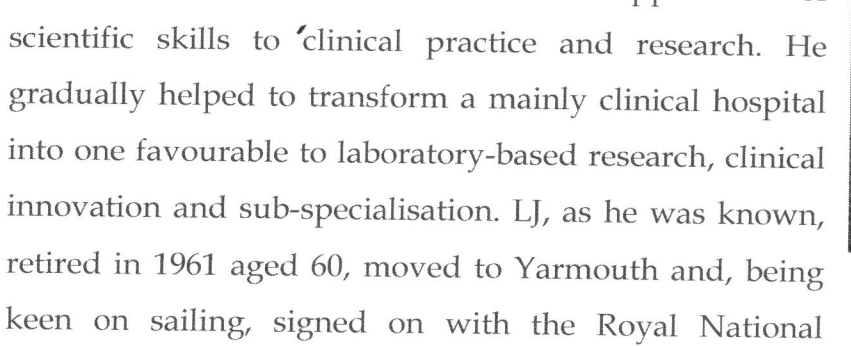

Arthur Kennedy[15]

Professor Davis died in 1980.[14]

References

[1]. Image courtesy of the Welcome Medical Library archive

[2]. The Royal: The History of Glasgow Royal Infirmary 1794 – 1994. Jacqueline Jenkinson, Michael Moss and Iain Russell. 1994

[3]. A Short History of Glasgow Royal Infirmary. John Patrick, 1940. Written for Colvilles magazine, Messrs Colvilles Ltd, Steel Manufacturer – Courtesy of Mr Alistair Tough, Archive Department, Mitchell Library, Glasgow.

[4]. Images courtesy of Andrew McAinsh and the Royal College of Physicians of Glasgow archive, 2018.

[5]. The Triple Qualification examination of the Scottish medical and surgical colleges, 1884-1993. Dingwall HM, J R Coll Physicians Edinb 2010; 40:269-276.

[6]. The Shaping of the Medical Profession. The History of the Royal College of Physicians and Surgeons of Glasgow, 1858-1999. Andrew Hull and Johanna Geyer-Kordesch, The Hambledon Press, 1999.

[7]. Images courtesy of Alistair Tough, Archive Department, Mitchell Library, Glasgow, 2018.

[8]. Image courtesy of Andrew McAinsh and the Royal College of Physicians of Glasgow archive, 2018

Bottom row from left to right: *Prof James Battersby, Prof Ian Murray, Prof Carstairs C Douglas (Dean, Anderson College of Medicine), Prof Andrew Allison (Dean, St Mungo's College of Medicine), Prof John Henderson, Prof John Graham.*

Second row from left to right: *Prof D MacKay Hart, Prof John A C Macewan, Prof A A Fitzgerald Peel, Prof A Muir Crawford, Prof William Rankin, Prof J R C Gordon, Prof Eric Oastler, Prof David Fyfe Anderson.*

Third row, third from right – *Dr Henry Withers Gray, father of the Blog author.*

Fourth row, third from left – *Dr Robert McPherson Cross, uncle of the Blog author.*

[9]. Dr Henry W Gray, personal reflection and collection

[10]. Reproduced with the permission of the National Library of Scotland
http://www.maps.nls.uk/index.html

[11]. Obituary. Walter King Hunter. The Lancet Nov 22, 1947. Accessed 11th May 2018.
https://ac.els-cdn.com/S0140673647908003/1-s2.0-S0140673647908003-main.pdf?_tid=8dff450d-7153-4f32-b42b-14c7c6986aa4&acdnat=1526029794_21699e005de5c0e9b7a36105fecba73f

[12]. Obituary for Dr Joseph Houston Wright
http://munksroll.rcplondon.ac.uk/Biography/Details/4905

[13]. Obituary. Archibald Wilson Harrington. British Medical Journal, July 18, 1953. Accessed 11th May, 2018.
https://www.bmj.com/content/2/4828/152.5

[14]. Leslie John Davis: Lives of the Fellows of the Royal College of Physicians, accessed February 23, 2018.
http://munksroll.rcplondon.ac.uk/Biography/Details/118

[15]. Image courtesy of Craig Richardson and Medical Illustration at GRI.

Chapter 6

A New Era for Women

For decades, prior to the momentous turn of events of 1888 which heralded the opening of the St Mungo's College of Medicine at Glasgow Royal Infirmary, women aspiring to become medical practitioners had experienced nationwide discrimination from the governing bodies in medicine.[1] It was not so much a 'glass ceiling' but 'the complete absence of a floor'. **Elizabeth Blackwell** was the first woman ever to receive a medical degree in 1849 from Geneva Medical College in New York State. This was one of the few establishments in the US that took women medical students and she required perseverance and tenacity to succeed. In the United Kingdom, some women had to use subterfuge to succeed in their training. Dr **James (Miranda) Barry** was a physician who qualified from Edinburgh in 1812 and rose to become Inspector General of Hospitals of the British Army. It was only on Barry's death in 1865, that her deception was discovered. Some pioneers like **Elizabeth Garrett Anderson** managed to use a loophole in the regulations of 'The Worshipful Society of Apothecaries' of London in 1865 and with some private training thrown in, qualified from the Society and obtained registration with the General Medical Council (GMC). She was prevented from obtaining a post in hospital, however, so after a medical degree

Elizabeth Garrett Anderson

at the Sorbonne in Paris in 1870, she simply set up her own successful clinic in London. The male medical establishment of the Society immediately closed the path taken to registration with the GMC by Garrett Anderson and it was not until 1876 that an Enabling Act of Parliament permitted women to enter medical training if the training establishments were in agreement but it was not compulsory. **Sophia Jex-Blake** had travelled to the USA in her early 20s and had been impressed by Dr **Lucy Ellen Sewall** a pioneer physician and one of the first women to graduate in medicine in that country. Looking to Scotland for enlightened attitudes to women students, Jex-Blake and six others were permitted to study at the University of Edinburgh. This was in separate 'ladies classes' in the early 1870s but there were issues when the ladies performed as well as the men in the class. Regrettably, they were given an uncomfortable time by the student body. The medical establishment closed ranks and refused to permit their graduation in 1873. The women were awarded a Certificate of Proficiency rather than a medical degree. They had to travel abroad for training and Jex-Blake was awarded her MD from the University of Berne in 1877. She also sat and passed the Dublin examination of Kings and Queens College of Physicians of Ireland. This Licence permitted her to register with the GMC. Jex-Blake later founded the short-lived '**School of Medicine for Women**' in Edinburgh in 1886.

Lucy Ellen Sewall

Sophia Jex-Blake

An early attendee at the 'School of Medicine for Women' in Edinburgh was a twenty-two year old **Elsie Maud Inglis**. She, and six other students including **Georgina** and **Grace Cadell**, rebelled against Jex-Blake's methods and set up a short-lived college of medicine to rival their erstwhile tutor. They were eventually forced to come West to Glasgow Royal Infirmary, it's Dispensary and the St Mungo's School of Medicine for 18 months to complete their practical training under Sir William Macewen. Inglis passed the Triple Qualification in 1892, and in 1894, opened a maternity hospital in Edinburgh for poor women called 'The Hospice' which was a forerunner of the **Elsie Inglis Memorial Hospital**. She eventually graduated MB.ChM from Edinburgh University in 1899, the

Elsie M Inglis[2]

same year that it opened its medical course to women. In 1914, the UK Government rejected her plans for an all women, front-line hospital unit, presumably for reasons of gender. Undaunted, she went on to lead a Scottish Women's Hospital Team of doctors and nurses to Serbia for the French Government and eventually suffered imprisonment. This gave her celebrity status and her courage, skill and endeavour were universally lauded in Britain.

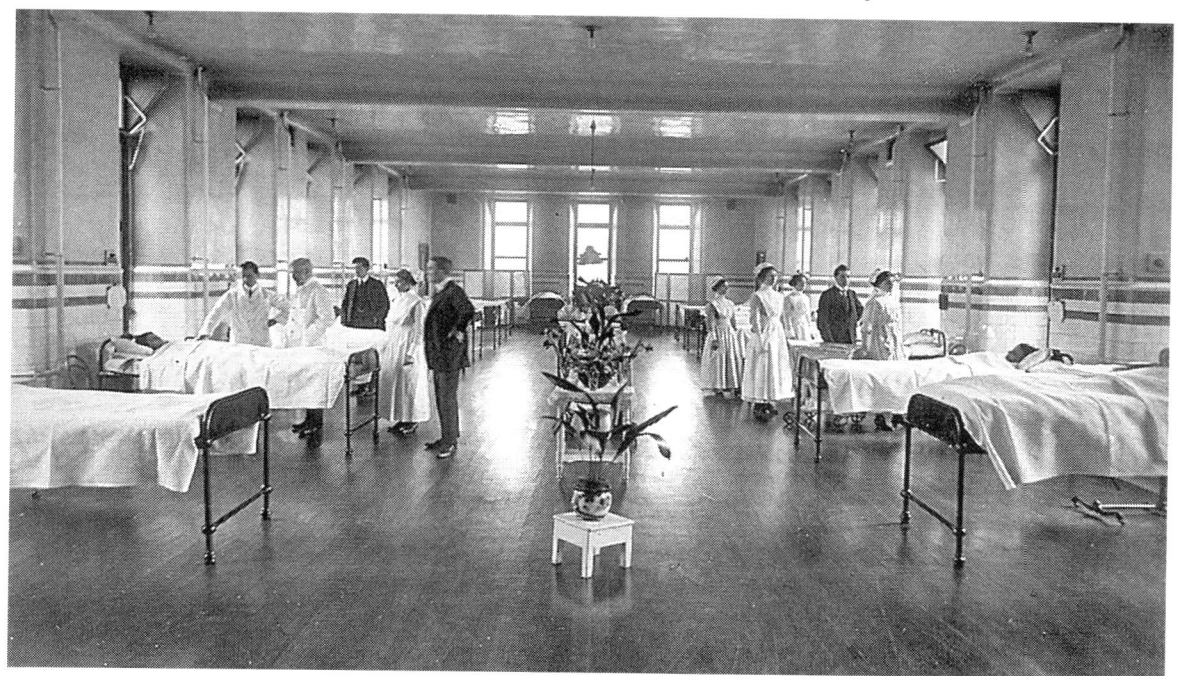

A West Medical Ward in the Adam Block[3]

Having been repatriated, she eventually took another all woman unit to Russia, this time with permission of the War Office. Inglis was a revolutionary at heart and became the Secretary of the Scottish Federation of Woman's Suffrage Societies. Her contribution has been belatedly honoured in 2018 by having her name etched on the plinth of the **Millicent Fawcett** statue in Parliament Square, London, as a crucial supporter of universal suffrage. Inglis died in 1917.

In the years 1884-9, 819 (96.5%) males passed the Triple Qualification (TQ) and 30 (3.5%) females while from 1890 to 1899, 2,136 (93.3%) males and 157 (6.8%) females were successful. On average, until the Universities took over all undergraduate training in 1946, about 7% of the medical class for the TQ was female. It is estimated that overall, about 50% of those sitting the TQ were successful. The first successful woman to pass the Scottish TQ was **Alice Ker** who received her diploma on 30th July, 1886[4]

Women medical staff of GRI around 1904 – reference to names[5]

Subsequently in 1889-92, the Universities of Glasgow, Edinburgh and London opened up registration for medical courses to women though for some years, classes were separate from the male students. **Queen Margaret College**, the University of Glasgow's higher education establishment for women, opened in 1883 and introduced a medical curriculum in 1890 with the financial backing of **Isabella Elder**, a local philanthropist. Classes in medicine began with 13 students in the winter of 1890/91. GRI was the only teaching hospital that accepted women for classes in clinical medicine and pathology at that time. However, as was the norm for the day, all classes were separated by gender. There was a hostile reaction at the gender separation from male students who complained that females were being provided with better teaching in view of their smaller class sizes. It was a difficult time for the Board of St Mungo's College but eventually, the furore settled and teaching continued. Not long after, the classes amalgamated and gender was no longer an issue.

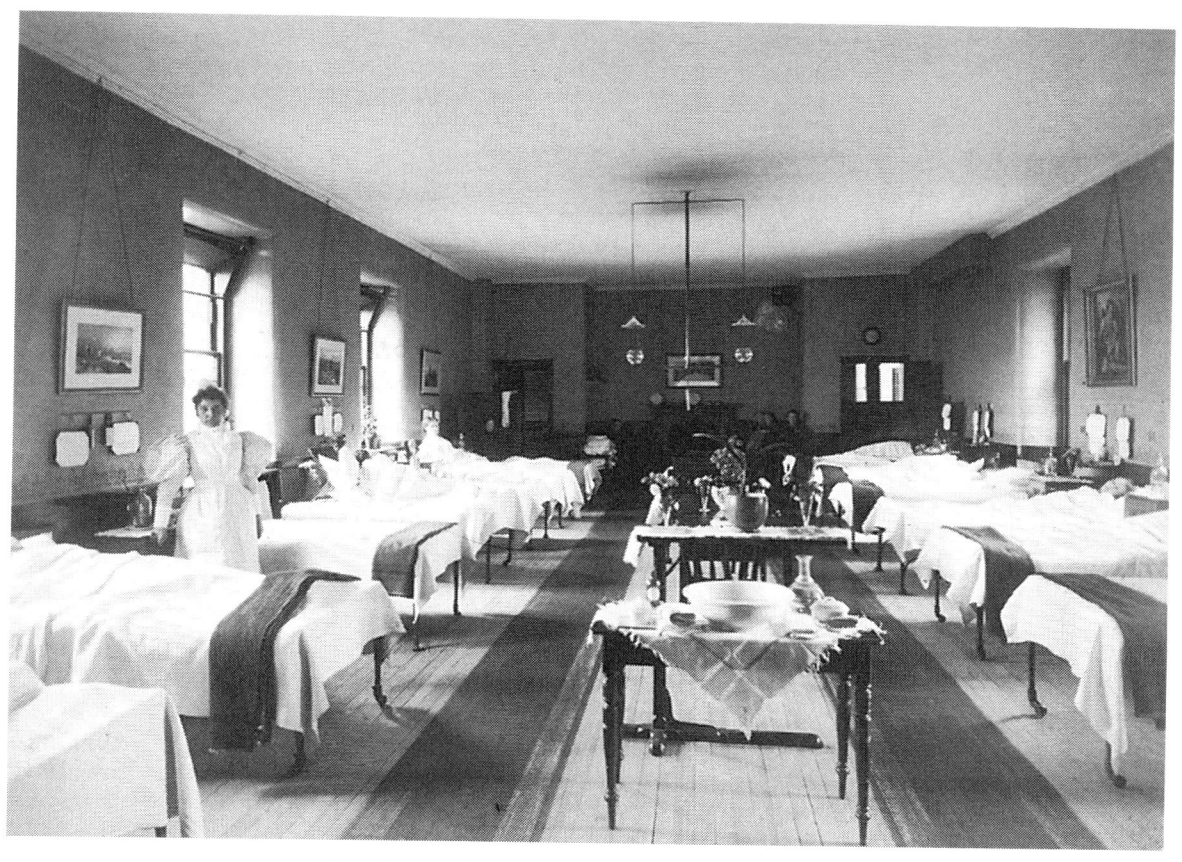

North Medical Ward in Adam Block[6]

The first ladies to graduate MB CM from Queen Margaret College were **Marion Gilchrist** and **Alice Louisa Cumming** in 1894. Both these ladies received their clinical training at GRI, as did most of the young women who followed in their footsteps. The first lady resident at GRI was **Marion Jamieson Ross** who graduated from Queen Margaret College in 1898. Women doctors were still barred from Fellowship of the Faculty of Physicians and Surgeons of Glasgow up till 1912. The first lady Fellow was **Yamani Sen,** a Licentiate in Medicine and Surgery of the University of Calcutta.

There were 25 women doctors registered with the GMC in 1881 in England and Wales and 495 in 1911. The reforms were beginning to affect the numbers of female doctors and when a shortage of male practitioners was experienced during World War 1, women were positively encouraged to consider medicine as a career.

The Dorcas Society

Beatrice Clugston was known for her compassionate and selfless work amongst the poor, sick and vulnerable women of Glasgow from the mid 1850s onwards.[7] While visiting a woman prisoner with cholera transferred to GRI in 1862, she was appalled by the conditions and struck by the lack of Christian women to visit, pray and comfort the sick in the wards. She also noted the lack of warm clothing for patients on discharge since their admission clothes were regularly incinerated to prevent re-infection. At the age of 35, she and a friend **Anne B Church** formed 'The Dorcas Society', a committee to organise the making of clothes for those discharged and this group was provided with a small room by Management. Teams of women were mobilised to make and repair clothing and visit patients in the wards. Struck by information about their poverty and conditions in their homes, Clugston began home visitation when indicated and liaised with doctors and nurses in the wards to provide the best circumstances for the patient upon discharge. This function eventually became the Almoner's Department and was the forerunner of the present day Medical Social Work Department. Beatrice Clugston organised for collections for the Society and regular donations to purchase material for the clothes. As President,

Beatrice Clugston

she also established convalescent homes in the West of Scotland and encouraged the development of similar services in other local hospitals.

Mrs **Mabel McKinley** joined the Dorcas Society as a ward visitor and worked in the clothes room at GRI. In 1942, she saw the need for refreshments for those waiting long hours at outpatient departments. Provided with a small room in the new outpatients department in the estate of the old Blind Asylum, which GRI had annexed, she provided initially a non-profit service for outpatients run by volunteers. As demand grew, the service required a nucleus of paid staff. 'Mabel MacKinlay's Tearoom' became an important part of the outpatient hospital visit and all profits went to the Dorcas Fund. This Fund supported and continues to support visitor facilities at GRI in the wards and outpatient departments.

Mabel McKinley

Posthumous Graduation

It is an interesting reflection on modern times with its emphasis on gender equality that Edinburgh University have just announced in early 2019, that Dr Jex-Blake and her 6 colleagues who were prevented from graduating in 1873 will be permitted to graduate posthumously in 2019. Presumably the Medical Faculty of 1869 were forward thinking in permitting the ladies to enter medical training but were unable to complete their vision due to pressure from other bodies. The current decision of the present day University Court will certainly correct a glaring injustice and will permit their families to celebrate 146 years later than planned.

References

[1]. Women and the Medical Professions. Lesley A. Hall
https://www.lesleyahall.net/wmdrs.htm

[2]. Images courtesy of Alistair Tough, Archive Department, Mitchell Library, Glasgow, 2018.

[3]. Images courtesy of Andrew McAinsh and the RCPSG archive

[4]. A Short History of Glasgow Royal Infirmary. John Patrick, 1940. Written for Colvilles magazine, Messrs Colvilles Ltd, Steel Manufacturer – Courtesy of Mr Alistair Tough, Archive Department, Mitchell Library, Glasgow.

[5]. Image courtesy of Alistair Tough, Mitchell Library Archives.
Sitting left to right: Margaret E Bryson, Agnes B Sloan, Jessica S MacEwan, Janet T Miller, Janet G Waddell.
Standing left to right: Gertrude D Bostock, Mary J Pirret, unknown male, Ethel McLelland, Alice Moorhouse.

[6]. Image courtesy of the Welcome Medical Library archive

[7]. Beatrice Clugston. A Life History.
http://www.mycityglasgow.co.uk/index_files/clugston.htm

Chapter 7

Nursing Comes of Age

Until the 1860s, nursing of the day attracted a largely unsuitable cohort of individuals who were often uneducated, malnourished, and untrained in the concept of cleanliness and hygiene. The job was open to all comers including unemployed female servants and widows forced to earn a living. Work was hard with the day shift starting at 6 am and finishing at 10 pm. As well as looking after patients with all that entailed, the nurses were effectively housekeepers with duties which included dusting, cleaning rooms, lighting fires, scrubbing toilet floors and washing down the long corridors and walls of wards. Many effectively lived and slept in rooms attached to the wards or in a building facing Castle Street, and North of the wards. Clearly, parents of able young women of sound character would consider hospital the last place when considering a career for their offspring.

Florence Nightingale in marble, GRI

The answer to this unacceptable nursing position at GRI came in the mid-1850s and had its origins 400 miles away in London. **Florence Nightingale** had battlefield experience of nursing during the Crimean war and had honed her considerable knowledge and skills in nursing, hygiene, sanitation,

The Lady with the Lamp, Hospital Chapel, GRI

hospital management and administration in that theatre of war. She saw a glaring need for nursing to become a profession by separating the cleaning from the caring, and by training the carers to a much higher standard. On her return from the Crimea, she founded the **Nightingale Training School** for Nurses at St Thomas' Hospital in 1860. The training espoused by Nightingale majored on compassion and commitment to the sick but also used an intelligent and diligent application of hospital administration to the issues of the day. This was revolutionary for its time and was occurring just as surgery, in particular, was increasingly requiring nursing staff versed in the techniques of infection control.

As a young widow aged 24 with a young child to support, **Rebecca Strong** was the 135th entrant to the Florence Nightingale School of Nursing in 1867. She completed the probationer training a year later and had further valuable experience working in the Military Hospital, Millbank, London and Winchester Hospital in Hampshire. She experienced the value of excellent bedside training and her insights into the expanding role of the nurse in hospital surgery and medicine allowed her to go on to pioneer nursing reform which had been unthinkable in the mid 19th Century. After a short spell as Matron of Dundee Royal Infirmary, she accepted the considerable challenge and became matron of GRI in 1879, the largest voluntary hospital in Scotland. The quality of nursing at GRI prior to 1879 was at low ebb and organised training was minimal. Lectures for nurses were arranged to provide training by the physicians and surgeons of the hospital, but they were often held in the evening. Even more inexplicably, the lectures were for

Rebecca Strong[1]

nurses who had just spent 14 hours on the wards. Rebecca Strong's ambition and overriding passion was to professionalise the craft of nursing by improving both the working conditions of nurses and their education and training. She constantly battled against the male dominated hospital culture of the time which saw nurses as pairs of hands fit only for the most menial of tasks. As a first stage, she persuaded the Board of GRI to buy new uniforms for her nurses to provide them with an 'Esprit de Corps' as well as a daily clean apron. She had many other changes in mind which would, step by step, increase both the knowledge and confidence of her staff in their own abilities and professionalism.

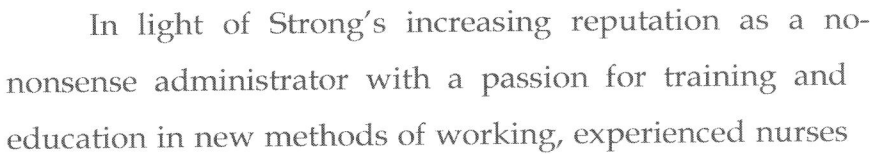

In light of Strong's increasing reputation as a no-nonsense administrator with a passion for training and education in new methods of working, experienced nurses

New Sister's Uniform, GRI, 1880

began to come to GRI from London, Edinburgh and from all over UK for further training. She had a redoubtable ally in William Macewen who always believed that nurses required more than basic training and education. Specifically, he thought that nurses required training in anatomy, physiology, therapeutics, medicine and surgery to enable them to understand the progression of disease and the treatment that could be provided. She was attracted by Macewen's approach to care during and following surgery and provided him with the most able of her probationers. Apparently, Macewen nurses became particularly loyal to the great man and even purchased a fish-kettle to enable him to sterilise his instruments before sterilisers became routinely available. Strong knew which young women became the best nurses and always insisted that the protection provided by a nurses home was essential for the health and welfare of younger nurses and for the success of any school of nursing. The Board of Management refused her initial request for a home but when she resigned to make her point, the Board eventually relented due to pressure from Macewen. In 1888, they built her a four-storey nurse's home that was separated from the Infirmary and

Phase 1 Nurse's Home in old building with Colonnade arrowed, 1888.
Phase two in the New Extension, 1910[2]

provided 88 bedrooms for nurses in training. The Home included bedrooms for superintendents, and on each floor, bathrooms, a sitting room, and access to a small kitchen area for brewing tea. Access to each floor was by a wide airy central staircase and rudimentary central heating was by hot water piping throughout. There was one recreation room and at the rear, a tennis court was built for the more athletic. The Home was linked to the hospital by a glazed covered way, 180 feet long and 15 feet wide, with an arched roof of glass also heated by hot water piping. This was known as the 'Colonnade' and provided shelter for nurses going to

Nurse Glass Covered Colonnade leading to Nurses Home[2]

and from the wards. It was also affectionately known as the 'Chicken Run' presumably because Matron could observe the comings and goings from her own flat in the Nurses Home in the evening. When the new Victoria Jubilee Medical Block was built and opened in 1914, Matron moved to a flat under the great dome on 6th floor. After her resignation in 1888 on a matter of principle, Strong had remained in Scotland, almost certainly on the advice of Macewen. Three years later in 1891 when she was re-appointed Matron, she could now reassure the families of young women entering nursing school of their security and that living and working conditions and indeed salaries were improving. The Nurse's Home was overseen by home sisters or superintendents and cleaning undertaken by an army of housekeepers. Although the bedrooms were Spartan in character and quite basic, the lounges and community rooms were sumptuous with fine drapes, carpets, mahogany desks, tables and soft furnishings of high quality. The junior nurse had only to look around to see that she had joined a profession of significance and substance.

This Home was extended (Phase 2) with a separate building of similar size in 1910 with construction almost in line with that of Phase 1. In 1926 a Phase 3 Nurses Home was built on Wishart Street and could be accessed from the 1910 Phase 2 Home by a corridor and steps above the new laundry facility. Before the motorcar became popular, it was a secluded area close to the Necropolis and therefore used for sleeping during the day particularly by staff on night duty.

Walkway and the Wishart Street Phase 3 of Nurses Home, both arrowed[2]

The Belvidere Nurses Home out of the City centre also became available for those nurses on night duty after the NHS appeared in 1948.

Nurses Preliminary Training School

In 1893, the Board agreed that all probationer nurses should be required to produce evidence of educational attainment before their acceptance into the training programme. This was the first step towards nursing becoming a profession and with the support of Macewen, a 'Preliminary Training School for Nurses' (PTS) was established. This provided a systematic course of training conducted away from the wards and followed by an examination. Strong then developed the Block Apprenticeship programme where short periods of instruction in school were followed by periods of clinical practice in the wards. The Training School proper opened the same year with the support of the GRI Board and the practical assistance from St Mungo's Medical College which provided two courses of instruction for the pupil nurses. Firstly, 3 months of lectures in anatomy, physiology, and hygiene were followed by examination. A first stage pass permitted the pupil nurse to start training in medicine, surgery and practical nursing, again, which was followed by examination. The successful probationer nurse was then able to enter the hospital wards armed with this theoretical knowledge. Nurses were now receiving a more thorough and technical education at GRI than was available anywhere else in the United Kingdom. The Teaching Department

GRI Nurses Training School Crest, 1950[2]

Training Room for Nurses in Teaching Department 1950[2]

Training Room was on the top floor of the Administrative block and had oak desks that many a nurse would etch with the date that she had been there. The blackboard and chalk, images, exhibits and an epidiascope represented the information technology. With time, the numbers of nurses starting the course outnumbered the space and so a new building for the Teaching Department was constructed in McLeod Street opposite from Provand's Lordship. The professional training programme was highly successful and popular with able young women who wanted to nurse and with its more rigorous and theoretically based nursing education approach, was later adopted by other teaching hospitals in the UK and imitated worldwide.[23] Following 3 years basic training for a direct entrant, or 2 years after previous training in Fevers or Sick Children, the graduate was given a sterling silver GRI lapel badge with their name and unique GRI graduation number.

Nurses New Training Department on McLeod Street, 1963

They also received a certificate that permitted registration with the General Nursing Council, which was formed in 1919. Along with improvements in accommodation and training opportunities, remuneration also increased which provided nurses with a new status in the community.

Helen Cairns Cook graduates general nurse from GRI in 1924, number 661[3]

Nursing hours decreased from an average of 15 per day in 1870 to 11 hours in the 1890s and down further to 9 hours by the 1950s. By then, day staff ran the ward between 8am and 9pm. Some from 8am to 12 midday and then 4.30pm to

9pm, the so-called split shift, while others worked a straight 8am to 5pm. In the 1920s, each nurse had one day off each week but from the 1950s, this increased to two days. The nature of duties also changed with most domestic chores ending to permit each nurse to concentrate her efforts almost exclusively on patient care.

Rebecca Strong with her team of Assistant Matrons and Graduating Pupil Nurses 1900 in front of the South Door of the Adam Block[2]

In 1895, Mrs Strong addressed the Matrons of the London Teaching Hospitals to explain the advantages of her programme of education for the advancement of the profession. It is clear that she played a major role in hospital reform in the UK at that time and also provided a resource of well-trained nurses

Graduation of the 1924 probationer nurses at GRI with Miss M S Donaldson, OSS, Matron, in front of the Administrative Block of the new building[4]

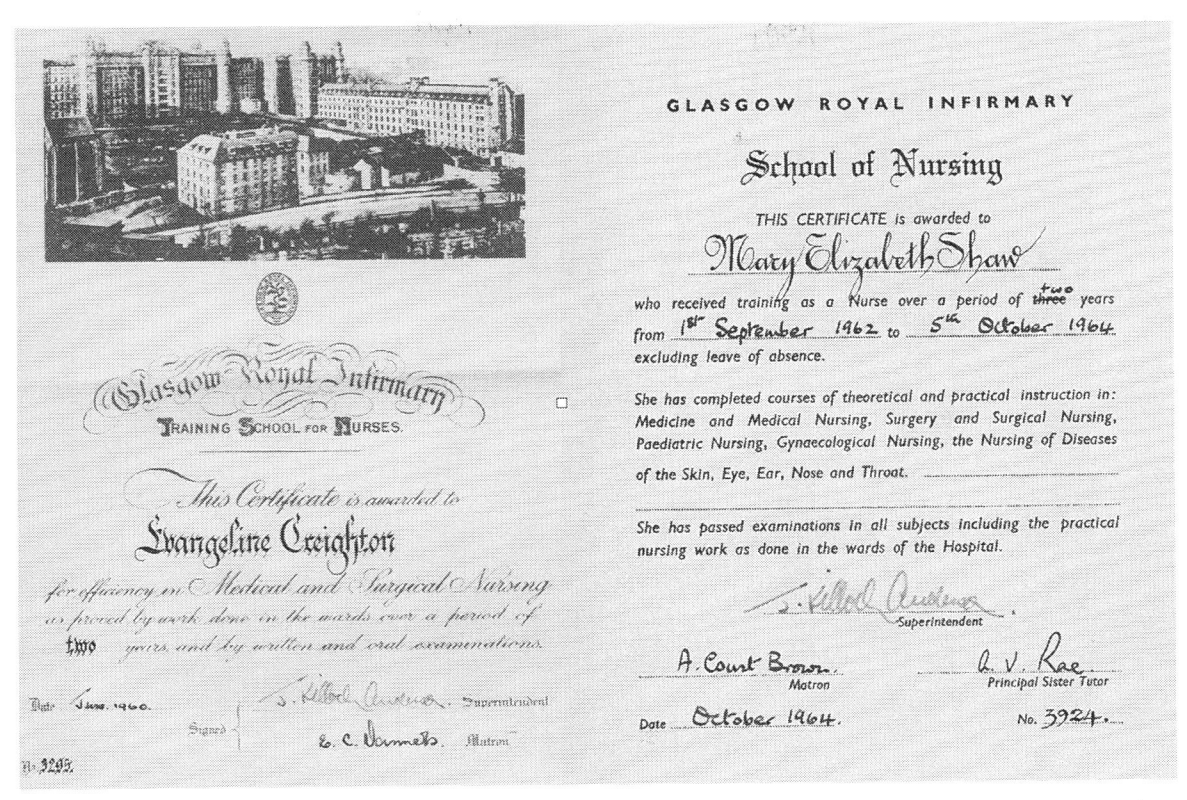

Two Individual Certificates Awarded at Completion of Training in 1960 and 1964[5]

upon whom the care of hospital patients in the UK, the Commonwealth and other Countries depended. A strict discipline was kept among nurses until the 1980s. This was considered a crucial aspect of preparation for team working and for character development and was reminiscent of the Services. Any nurse meeting Matron in the corridor would stand to one side, head bowed with arms crossed and cloak covering the uniform. This was known as 'fading' and was respected by the majority. Ward sisters took full responsibility for their ward, their staff and patients. Staff nurses attached to the ward would support Ward sister and supplement the training given by the Supervisors and training sisters for the enrolled nurses on the ward. More senior staff,

Pupil Nurse Uniform, 1900[2]

who were usually assistant Matrons or Superintendents, visited the wards once every day and three times during the night to be given a report on every patient.

Night sister also requested the ward temperature and once the visit was over, a knock on the pipes alerted the next ward to the imminent night visit. An early 'bush telegraph' system was in operation.

By the 1950s, night nurses wakened the patients at 6am and made tea, boiled eggs and toast from the ward kitchen or served porridge, bacon and scrambled egg made in the hospital kitchen. Nurses themselves were never permitted to eat or drink while on duty but served patients food from the centre of the ward onto trays that had been set up by the ward orderly. They then took the trays to the beds or tables for patients who were ambulant.

Nurses Dining Room, GRI 1950[2]

Ward nurses were given a short break in the morning and afternoon of 15 minutes and there were two sittings of 30 minutes for lunch and for the evening meal. During the day in the 1950s, nurses were required to stand behind their chairs in the dining room on the ground floor until Matron and her senior staff had taken their places at the top table. Only then would they be permitted to sit down and be served by dining room staff. By the 1960s, the set tables with flowers and water had been replaced by benches and bench seating. Self-service and informality was the new normality.

GRI Nurses Uniform, 1960[6]

Traditions varied between hospitals but GRI maintained a rigid policy on the uniform until it changed into more comfortable attire in the early 1980s. Uniform dress was of a standard length around mid-calf and the apron had to be of similar length. Black stockings were essential and for many years, the Glen Eagles Cuban rubber heeled shoes were 'de rigueur'.

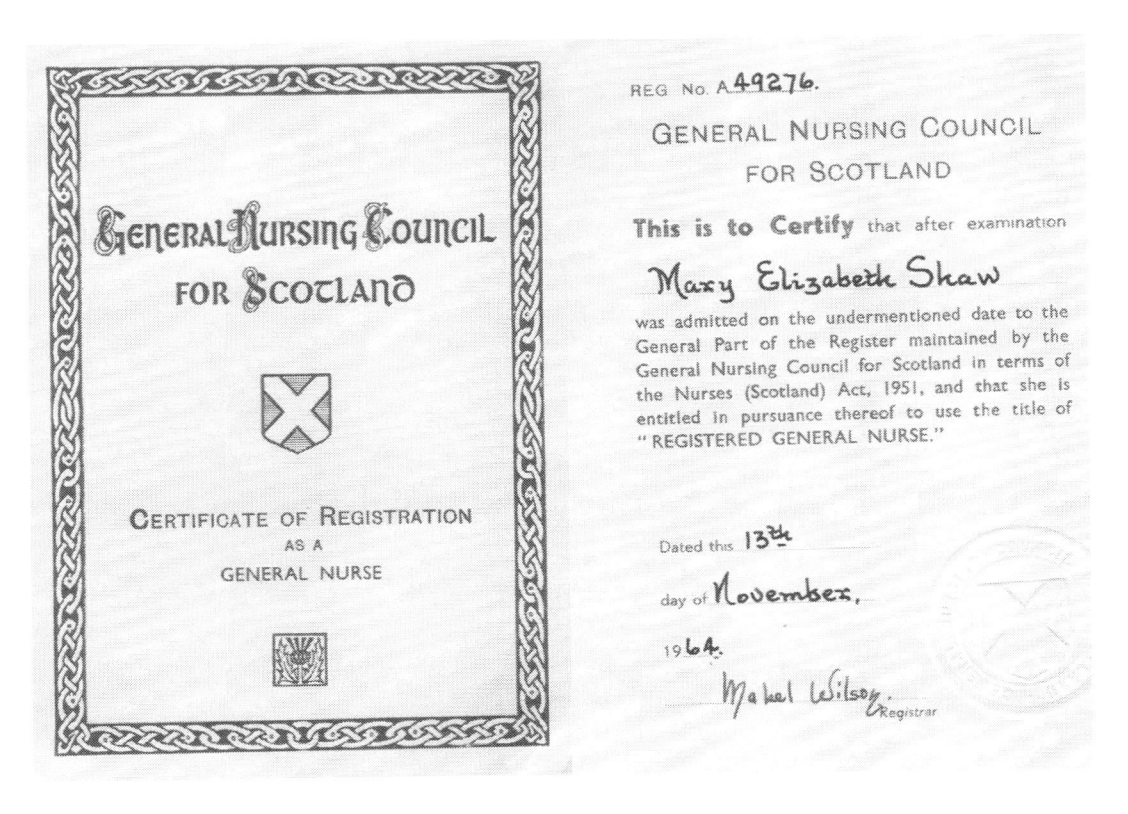

Certificate for Registered General Nurse, 1964[7]

Senior nursing staff who lived in the community were not permitted to wear their uniform outside of hospital because of the risk of infection to patients. There was a changing room with lockers in the nurse's home for those individuals. Caps could be difficult to position and fold correctly, especially the

Evangeline Creighton wearing 'wings' cap. Badge follows registration with Scottish Nursing Council, 1960[8]

'wings' cap of the staff nurses who were more senior. The starched collar was not a favourite.

In the wards, there were regular bed-making rounds, bedpan rounds, bed bathing rounds, medicine rounds, dressing rounds in surgery and weekly hair and nail inspection. During the weekly wall washing by ward maids, the beds were wheeled to the centre of the ward giving an opportunity for the floors to be polished with jocks. Jocks comprised a square of wood with flannel on the underside for the dried polish and a long handle to permit buffing of the floor. In the 1960s, electric powered 'buffers' became available. Until autoclaving of instruments became the norm, trays for instruments were 'flamed' with surgical spirit to sterilise the surface prior to a procedure round. While ward maids cleaned the WCs, toilet and sluice floors, nursing staff used the bedpan and urinal washers to clean and burnish the stainless steel for later inspection. Nurses would also collect and test the urine specimens nightly and arrange for sputum samples with patients as required.

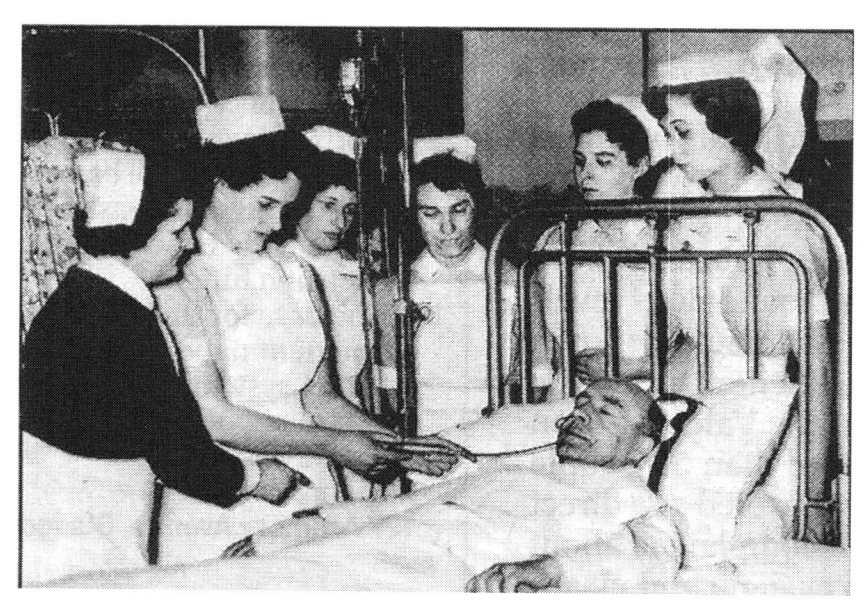

Sister Tweedlie Teaches at the Bedside 1960, with Staff Nurse (R) Wearing her 'Wings' Cap

Mrs Strong supported the State Registration of nurses that began in 1919. This compiled and maintained a Register of qualified nurses and enabled standards of discipline and practice to be maintained uniformly throughout the country. The Nurses (Scotland) Act also established a General Nursing Council which was responsible for inspecting and approving training courses. Following registration, the nurse was issued with a badge for her cap or uniform to confirm to the general public that she was on the register for general nursing or fevers. By formulating rules for nurse training and arranging for State examinations in the larger training centres, the Nursing Council improved and standardised general nursing qualifications throughout the country. In 1918 Strong helped found the Scottish Nurses' Club in Glasgow and in 1921 she was in the chair at the inaugural dinner for the Glasgow Royal Infirmary Nurses' League which continued to bring GRI nurses together for 88 years until the last gathering in 2009. The principal aims of the League were to promote the interests of the nursing profession, to engage in charitable enterprises within GRI and to forge links between GRI nurses past and present. Miss Jane **Melrose** became Matron on Rebecca Strong's retiral in 1903.

Preliminary Training School, Lancaster Crescent, Glasgow[2]

GRI witnessed this revolution in bedside nursing care first-hand and profited by it. A new PTS was purchased in the West end of Glasgow at 4-5 Lancaster Crescent with accommodation for 53 pupil student nurses and consisted of Lecture Rooms, a Practical Demonstration Room, a Demonstration Kitchen, a Laboratory, Sitting Room and Dining Room. Following the 3 months in PTS, the probationer spent 3 months in the wards of GRI before full acceptance for a further three and a half years training, two and a half as a pupil nurse and 1

Rebecca Strong O.B.E.[2]

year as a fully trained staff nurse permitted to wear her 'wings' cap. Not before time and aged 95, Rebecca Strong was awarded an O.B.E. in 1939 by the King at Buckingham Palace for services to nursing.

In the early post-war years, the **Wood Report** advised that student nurses be relieved of repetitive and non-nursing duties to enable basic training in 18 months which would permit a further 6 months of concentrated study in a speciality before registration. In the 1950s, GRI embarked upon an experiment in nurse training that would see essential theoretical and practical training completed in 2 years followed by a 3rd year of practical experience before registration. Apart from the integration of theoretical and practical instruction, the other objective was to establish the concept and practice of team working. This was a success and led to greater personal contact between patient and nurse and could be implemented by nurses in training. A further experiment in training in 1957 saw a streaming of the more educationally qualified probationers into a more academically oriented training to bring theory and practice together based in teaching premises on Cleveden Road, Glasgow. These 'Cleveden Ladies'[9] were, in fact, the first steps in Glasgow towards a degree course in nursing.

All Nurses stayed in the Nurses Home at GRI except when on night duty when, at the end or beginning of their shifts, they were either bussed to the Nurses Home at Belvidere Hospital for the more restful environment of the East end of

Nurses Home, Belvidere Hospital[10]

Glasgow on the banks of Clyde or were given a room in the quieter Phase 3 Annex of the Nurse's Home on Wishart Street. The University of

Edinburgh had a degree course in nursing studies from around 1960 but it was the recommendation of the **Briggs** Report in 1972 that brought graduate training in nursing to the fore in Glasgow. Under the guidance of Professor Edward McGirr who was Dean of the Faculty of Medicine, a joint committee of Greater Glasgow Health Board and the University of Glasgow (UG) agreed to set up the first four year course in Glasgow for an ordinary degree in nursing combining academic study and professional training. The graduates were also recognised by the General Nursing Council of Scotland for registration as a general nurse.

Phase 3 Nurses Home (L) on Wishart Street from the Necropolis. Laundry Centre and older Nurses Homes (R) [2]

From the 1980s, nurses at GRI have increasingly become an integral part of the care package with autonomies of action within the medical or surgical teams. The Nurse's Homes stopped being used for probationer nurses when the GRI College of Nursing closed and were gradually turned over to other hospital activities such as clinics and offices. The Caledonian University of Glasgow (CUG) began their Diploma course in nursing when the North College of Nursing based at GRI closed in 1996. The course became a degree course at CUG in 2012 finally completing the desire of Rebecca Strong to professionalise all branches of nurse training.

Rachel Wylie who had been sister in ward 37, became the last traditional Matron of GRI between 1975 and 1989.

Reference

[1]. Rebecca Strong account: Nightingales after Nightingale.
http://www.kingscollections.org/exhibitions/archives/from-microbes-to-matrons/matrons-nurses-and-nursing/nightingales-after-nightingale

[2]. Images courtesy of Alistair Tough, Archive Department, Mitchell Library, Glasgow, 2018.

[3]. Images courtesy of Evangeline and Sam Creighton

[4]. Graduation of probationer nurses in 1924 including the mother of Dr John A Thomson, author of this Blog, 7th from left, second back row, Miss Margaret Provan.

[5] Images courtesy of Evangeline Creighton and May Gray MBE

[6]. Image courtesy of Craig Richardson and the Medical Illustration Department at Glasgow Royal Infirmary.

[7]. Image courtesy of May Gray MBE

[8]. Image courtesy of Evangeline Creighton

[9]. Mrs Morag Doust (Nee Fulton), personal recollection

[10]. Belvidere Nurses Home used by Glasgow Royal Nurses from 1950
https://canmore.org.uk/site/172494/glasgow-london-road-belvidere-hospital-nurses-home-and-administrative-block

Chapter 8

The Auld Hoose

In the 19th Century, the GRI as an Institution played a major role in maintaining the health of the citizens of Glasgow. Real anxiety and disquiet in Glasgow became apparent when the Board of Management made the decision to replace the well-loved Adam building. This was not really surprising such had been the aura surrounding the building and the awe and esteem held for the work done within its walls. There was no better site for reconstruction and so all were agreed that GRI would be rebuild on the same site

John Freeland Fergus[1]

Dr **John Freeland Fergus** graduated MA at Glasgow in 1883, MB in 1888 and MD in 1897. He had been a resident at GRI in 1889 and reflected this mood of sadness yet one also of expectation when he penned the following poem called 'The Auld Hoose'[2]. He followed the ballad style first popularised by **Carolina**

Oliphant (**Lady Nairne** 1766 – 1845) in her own poem 'The Auld Hoose' which is still sung today within the Scottish folk lexicon and is a pipe tune air.

The Auld Hoose

(The old Royal Infirmary of Glasgow)

Oh, the Auld Hoose, the Auld Hoose,
That noo they're pu'in doon,
Mair than a hunner years it's been
The glory o' the toon;
The memories that round it cling
Are sweet as flo'ers in May;
But the Auld Hoose, the Auld Hoose,
It's passing fast away

Oh, the Auld Hoose, the Auld Hoose,
What though the wards were wee;
Nae better wark than there was done
We couldna wish to see.
And, oh, the leal and kindly hearts,
That through the lang, lang years
Wi' pity tended on the sick
Or soothed the dyings' fears.

Oh, the Auld Hoose, the Auld Hoose,
What names it can reca';
But Lister's, a' folks maun aloo,
Maist glorious o' them a';
His name's a treasured memory
That lives in every stane;
And still will live, although ere lang
The Auld Hoose will be gane.

Oh, the Auld Hoose, the Auld Hoose,
Beside the auld High Kirk,
Fu' mony a cheerin' beam it's thrown
Ower a' the city's mirk;
The radiant light that frae it
streams, Will aye haud on to burn;

Although the dear Auld Hoose itsel'
To dust and ashes turn.

Oh, the Auld Hoose, the Auld Hoose,
Sae couthy, kind and bein;
Where stately ye ha'e stood sae lang,
Ye'll be nae langer seen;
But frae your ruins, born again,
The New Hoose springs to life;
Full armed, with death and dread disease
to wage a noble strife.

Oh, the New Hoose, the New Hoose,
We wish it a' success,
That Heaven may aye upon it smile
And God its labours bless;
The New Hoose, the New Hoose,
It's big and braw and high;
But, oh, it's chiefest glory is
That it's the GRI.

John Freeland Fergus (1865 – 1943)

Glasgow Royal Infirmary was an important lifeline for the citizens of Glasgow from 1794. Although a voluntary hospital reliant upon fees for admission, it's policy was to admit emergencies without a requirement for payment. This engendered universal admiration, honour and esteem for GRI as an organisation among the surrounding populace. It is unsurprising that this would happen among predominately poor social groupings since upon admission to a warm, clean bed and being provided with 3 meals each day, many would feel they had been sent to heaven. The population admired and supported the work done in ways that are almost unthinkable in our present day NHS where, more commonly, one finds a culture of entitlement. John F Fergus who wrote 'The Auld Hoose', a ballad about the first Glasgow Royal, also penned his deeper thoughts on the Institution called the GRI using Biblical allegory[2]. He used his experience of its many patients and staff to capture the love and almost veneration for the Institution that, for some, represented the nearest place to 'Holy Ground'.

The Auld Hoose

(The Spirit of the GRI)

More than a hundred years have rolled
Since near God's House it raised it's head
A house of hope, of life, of love
Beside the dwelling of the dead.
There stand the twain – the Almighty's fane
Where lie the dead in hallowed ground?
This shrine of suffering – and in both
The Spirit of the Lord is found.

For not in temples made with hands
Doth God alone delight to dwell;
The humble, reverent, searching heart
The world's great Master pleaseth well.

The Hymn of human thankfulness,
That rises hence throughout the years,
Strikes sweeter far than incensed praise
Upon the Almighty's listening ears.

The higher that the temple stands
The deeper is the quarry riven;
From pain's dark depths were hewen the stones
That raise this temple nearer heaven.
And who the builders? Look around
If you their multitude would see –
The sick, the halt, the lame, the blind,
Poor brethren of adversity

Each bringing to the destined place
The polished stones of thankful praise,
That, slowly garnered through the years,

*At length the perfect fabric raise
Which stands unblemished in its strength,
And still shall stand while ages roll,
Firm – braced against the shocks of time
By stanchions of the human soul.*

*What of the ministrants who wait
Within the temples sacred walls,
To whom, to serve its holy courts
The Spirit of the Master calls?
"Unto the least, unto the least",
Although perchance their service be,
Yet rings the verdict from on high,
"Yea verily, 'tis unto Me."*

*A splendid heritage is theirs
Descended thru untarnished years
Of tiredness, toil, of scorned delights,
Laborious days of hopes and fears;
A heritage of lustrous names,
Of honoured worth, of high desire,
And theirs the treasured privilege,
To tend with care the sacred fire.*

*Which ever burns with steady flame
Amid the whirlwind rush of life,
Unflickering 'mid the clang of toil,
Unwav'ring 'mid the market's strife;
Serene and calm it sheds its light
O'er spots of darkness, like the star
That long ago in Eastern skies
The shepherds worshipped from a far.*

*And still the self-same message comes
As with the primal portend then,
Of peace on earth, of joy in heaven,
Glory to God, goodwill to men;
And still celestial shapes appear
For all the wondering earth to see,
The angel forms of steadfast Faith,
Of Hope and Blessed Charity.*

*Heaven knows how many feet have trod
The dark Gethsemane of pain,
And who shall say what weary ones
Must pace its pathways yet again;
But from this temple's open door
There stretches forth a radiant light,
Cheering their path, and leading on
These suffering pilgrims of the night.*

*If to a Calvary – their cross
Seems lightened by the wondrous rays;
Or, if with, stronger step they pass
Back to men's busy haunts and ways,
They bear with them across the years
Where'er Life's toilsome path they trace,
Some shining radiance, faint or bright
Of the Shekinah of this place.*

John Freeland Fergus (1865 – 1943)

References

[1]. Image courtesy of Andrew McAinsh and the Royal College of Physicians of Glasgow archive, 2018.

[2]. Fancies of a Physician: verses medical and otherwise, in Scots and English. John F Fergus; Brown, Son and Ferguson, Glasgow, 1938.

Entrance to the Electric Pavilion, ground floor of Lister Block, 1902[1]

Chapter 9

Electricians Spark Change

The late 19th Century was a fertile period for science and the atomic theory in particular. It had been almost 80 years since **John Dalton** proposed that atoms were the smallest division of matter. In 1875, **William Crookes**, an English chemist and physicist, found cathode rays in his electrified discharge tube with partial vacuum when high voltage was applied to the electrodes.

William Crookes

In 1887, **Joseph John Thomson**, an English physicist, repeated the experiment and found that the cathode rays of William Crookes, **Johann Wilhelm Hittorf** and others were, in fact, negatively charged sub-atomic particles by changing their path with positive charge or with magnetic fields. The particles were later called electrons.

J J Thomson

In November 1895, **Wilhelm Röntgen**, Professor of Physics at Würtzburg University, found an unknown radiation when he passed a current through a Crookes – Hittorf tube. Serendipitously, he noticed a glow on a nearby screen painted with fluorescent barium platinocyanide which was unrelated to his experiment. To his surprise, the glow persisted when light was excluded by paper and wood but not by lead

Wilhelm Röntgen

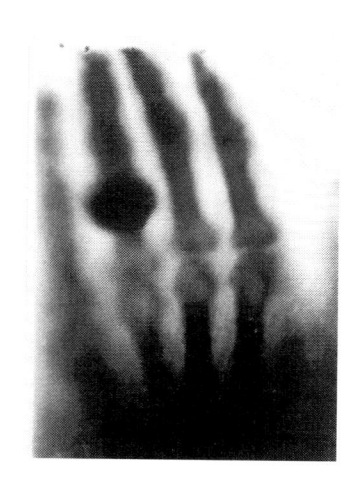

First X-ray, 15 min exposure

sheeting. Putting a hand in the beam, he found that his bones became opaque but not the soft tissue and that he could record the 'shadow images' with a photographic plate normally reserved for light. Röntgen called the emanations X-rays, because they were unknown in character. Presumably to please his wife **Anna Bertha**, he obtained a photographic X-ray plate of her hand after a 15-minute exposure.[1] This has become an iconic image. He was awarded the first Nobel Prize in physics and, like Pierre Curie, Röntgen refused to take out patents relating to his discovery. He wanted society to benefit from its application to the health and welfare of mankind.

The excitement in the scientific community was intense and the news of the discovery of X-rays reached the UK during the first week of January 1896. Röntgen had sent a copy of his paper to **William Thomson**, Lord Kelvin who was fascinated and keen to follow up the discovery. Lord Kelvin arranged to demonstrate X-rays on the 5th February 1896 at the Royal Philosophical Society of Glasgow. He was unwell on that date so asked his nephew, **James Thomson Bottomley**, an Irish born physicist, to demonstrate the X-rays for him. Lord Kelvin loaned the apparatus to Bottomley including Crookes tubes specially blown for him and asked his two friends, Lord **Blythswood** who was a notable amateur scientist and **John Macintyre**, who was consultant electrician in charge of the Electrical Department of Glasgow Royal Infirmary, to support Bottomley in the demonstration. The meeting was held in the Electrical Department of the Infirmary and during it, Macintyre convincingly showed the assembled body a needle in a wrist using the new X-ray technology. This demonstration was the first use of X-rays in a Scottish

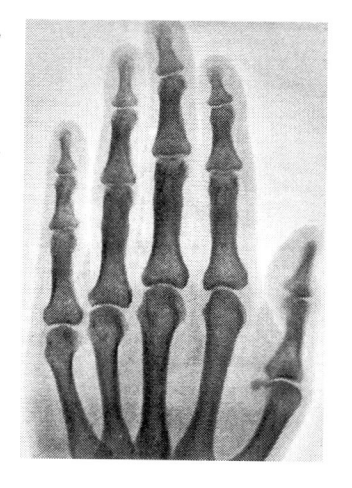

John Macintyre hand, 3 min exp[2]

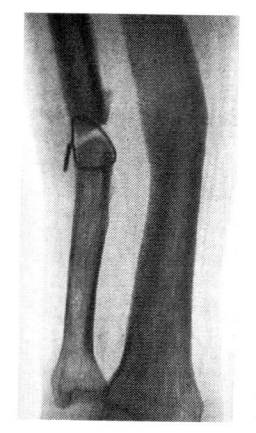

Ununited Fracture[2]

106

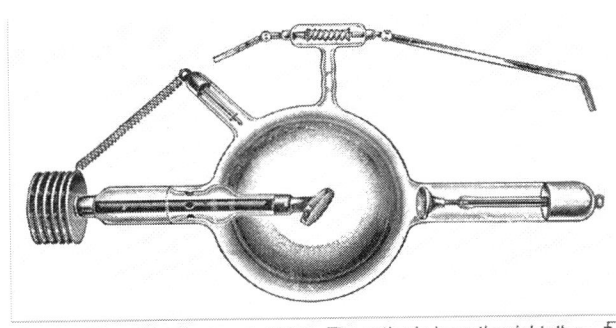

Crookes X-ray tube from early 1900s. The cathode is on the right, the anode is in the center with attached heat sink at left. The electrode at the 10 o'clock position is the anticathode. The device at top is a 'softener' used to regulate the gas pressure.

hospital[2]. Macintyre quickly added a new X-ray 'photography' or 'skiagraphy' section to his Electrical Department in March 1896 and this became the first ever X-ray Department in any hospital although within the year, most in the UK had followed suit. He experimented with the technology using a pallet with a Crook's tube suspended over it connected to an unshielded control panel. Four weeks later, he showed the image (a Skia) of a larynx. Enthused by the possibilities, Macintyre went on in the year to demonstrate abnormal hearts, a diseased hip joint, a coin in the gullet and a kidney stone. He was the first to demonstrate cineradiology in 1897 and used a moving frog's leg. Later, he showed X-ray images of the movements of the knee and later, of the stomach after a Bismuth meal with the same technology. All large hospitals in Scotland had X-ray facilities in the electrical Dpt within the year.

John Macintyre[3]
LLD.DL. FRSE. MIEE.

John Macintyre trained as an electrical engineer in the 1870s just at that moment in history when the gas lighting of Glasgow streets would start to be replaced by its electrical equivalent. A bequest from an aunt permitted him to study medicine at the University of Glasgow and he graduated MB with commendation in 1882. Macintyre gained experience in London, Paris and Vienna before returning to Glasgow as an expert in conditions affecting voice production and it's recording on phonograph wax cylinders. As specialist in voice disorders, many famous singers such as Ignacy Paderewski, Joseph Conrad, and Dame Nellie Melba sought his advice in his private rooms in Bath Street, Glasgow where he examined them and recorded their voices. At

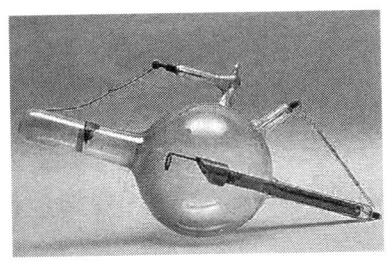

Early Vacuum X-ray tube[3]

the GRI, he became a demonstrator in Anatomy at St Mungo's Medical School,

Early string galvanometer for ECG from Cambridge Analytica 1916

and was appointed assistant surgeon for diseases of the nose and throat in 1886 then 7 years later, consultant surgeon. In view of his previous experience and training, Macintyre also became consulting medical electrician to GRI in 1887 and ran the new and expanding 'Department for the Application of Medical Electricity'. At this point, he would probably have supervised the electrification of wards and theatres at GRI. Macintyre also lectured in diseases of the nose and throat to Anderson's College Medical School.

In 1887, Macintyre ran the Department which brought together the diverse areas of medicine where electricity and electrodes could be

Gaiffe and Blythswood Static Machines for therapy[5]

used in diagnosis and treatment. His first published on a new apparatus for looking into the larynx or mouth and this was the first electrical or battery illuminated endoscope.[4] In the department, he also supervised the new electrocardiograph, which required a string galvanometer to produce a photographic image of the electrical activity of the heart. Eventually, he found private funding to connect all the medical wards by cable so that galvanometer images of the ECG could be received remotely from the bedside.

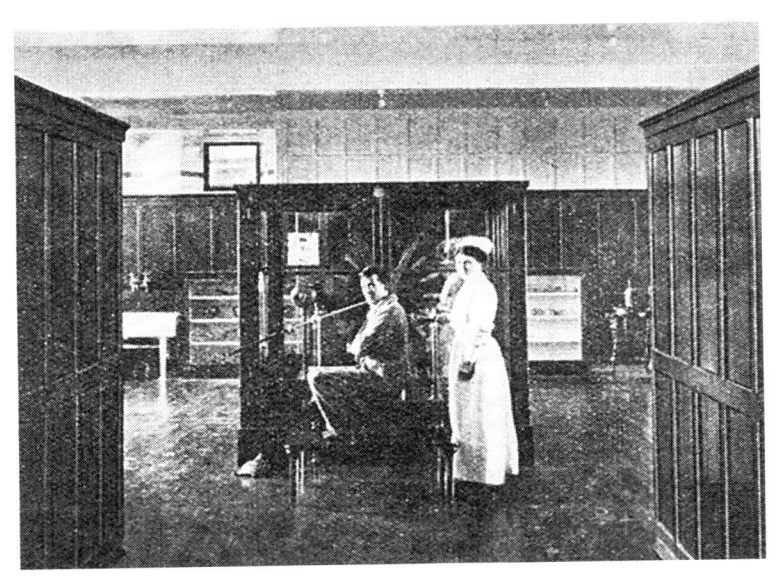

Entrance to Macintyre's Electrical ward[6]

Other special areas in this electrical department included different forms of diathermy treatments for ablation, electrotherapeutic equipment for diagnosis of nerve or muscle diseases, and static electrical treatment for sciatic pain. An incandescent light bath for skin diseases, high frequency current therapy for those with muscular or nervous afflictions and, Finsen's light therapy for Lupus Vulgaris (Tuberculosis of the skin) completed the list.

As he demonstrated the power and scope of the new X-ray modality in 1896 for the first time, Macintyre immediately saw its transforming potential for medical and surgical diagnosis. The visual

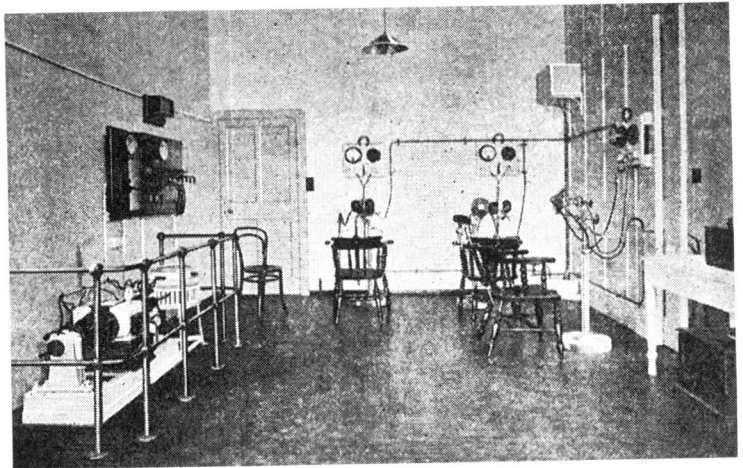

Transformer and Light Therapy Room[7]

probing of the dark recesses of the body would permit bone disease, foreign bodies, tumours and infections to become readily visible. The Managers of the

Board of GRI and the Medical Superintendent supported this major advance wholeheartedly and provided larger premises and extra staff for the venture.

The Department had been previously set up for electrical work including the mains electricity connection from the Glasgow Corporation and therefore required

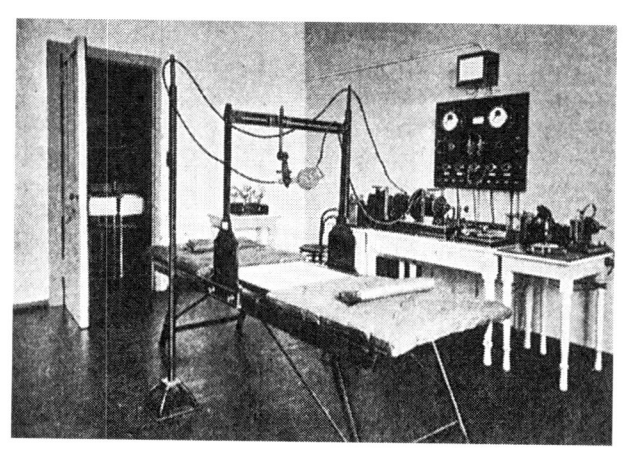

For recumbant X-rays. Note X-ray vacuum tube[7]

only tweaks to provide the voltages necessary for the vacuum tubes. Both visiting and Dispensary staff began using the technology for diagnosis and throughput increased year on year.

Because of his past electrical training, Macintyre was aware of the pitfalls in the use of mains electricity and took great steps to avoid them. Firstly, was the danger to patients from high voltage electricity itself. The Department was arranged so that it was impossible for high currents from 500 or 250 Volt Direct Current supplied by the Glasgow Corporation to touch the patients using the apparatus. He used his electrical experience of the safety measures required so that mains electricity only drove the generator motors or transformers, which then turned the dynamos that in turn, powered the apparatus for the patients. This

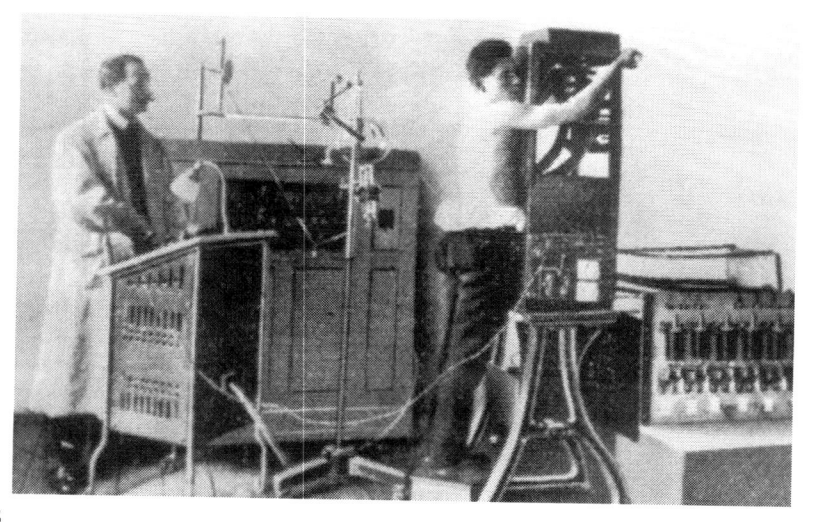

Early Apparatus for Chest X-ray with X-ray Vacuum Tube[7]

ensured that there was always a break between outside power and inside usage by apparatus. Secondly, the dangers to doctors, and nursing staff of over exposure to X-rays were increasingly reported within the medical community.

Macintyre's New Electrical Pavilion, 1902[5]

For example, a radiologist called **Francis Hull-Edwards** required amputation of his left arm and others developed carcinoma of the skin or leukaemia. Macintyre experimented with his hand as a 'penetrometer' and this resulted in an early burn. It took decades before the specific standards for permissible doses for staff were set, but by then, there had been an alarming attrition rate of radiologists inadvertently exposed to excessive doses of X-rays, the so-called radiation martyrs. Having experienced the minor burn to his skin early on, Macintyre developed sensible safety measures protecting the medical, technical and nursing staff in his department and introduced lead gloves and aprons.

X-ray Cinematographic Imaging Apparatus[6]

The Board of GRI continued to support all of Macintyre's endeavours to innovate with the X-ray technology of

111

the day. The new 'Electric Pavilion' opened in the ground floor of the Lister building in 1902. All rooms were lit by the 250-volt circuit from the Glasgow Corporation and a transformer provided 55 volts and 50 amps from the Corporation supply for the equipment. In case the Corporation supply failed, a gas engine with dynamo provided 56 volts and 30 amps. Large coils were added to provide the high voltage necessary for the X-ray tubes. Fluorescent screening became important for bowel investigation as the equipment improved and radiation doses could be minimised to patient and staff. Macintyre experimented with cinematographic imaging from early on[6] and usually imaged with 24 photographic plates over six seconds. By reducing the size of the large photographic film, rapid sequential visualisation of the smaller plates permitted him to show moving images of heart, limbs or bowel. The term 'Stereoscopic photography' was added to permit localisation of foreign bodies. Single X-ray plates of chest or skeleton in anterior or posterior position increased in number almost exponentially and Macintyre found the workload oppressive. The Board again stepped in and Dr **James Robertson Riddell** was employed as medical electrician in 1902 having been an assistant since 1899. Riddell supervised the establishment of X-ray departments in the Eye Infirmary, The Royal Hospital for Sick Children and the Royal Alexandra Infirmary, Paisley and became fulltime at the Western Infirmary in 1920. Dr **Capie** and Dr **Katherine Chapman** joined as assistants in 1906 with Dr Chapman becoming a medical electrician/radiologist in 1920. By this time, Macintyre had five medical operators and a large staff of nurses. The **George Fifth Electrical Institute** opened in the basement of the new Jubilee Medical Block on 7th July 1914. Thanks to the generosity of the citizens of Glasgow, the equipment including vacuum tubes was all purchased without the hospital having to expend its scarce funds.

From 1903, Macintyre was also involved in the treatment of skin cancers with radiation using X-rays and the expensive element radium.[8] The element was so scarce that he was a member of the Radium Committee of 1914 in Glasgow which attempted to share the scarce resource between the three Infirmaries, The Royal Samaritan Hospital for Women and The Royal Cancer Hospital.

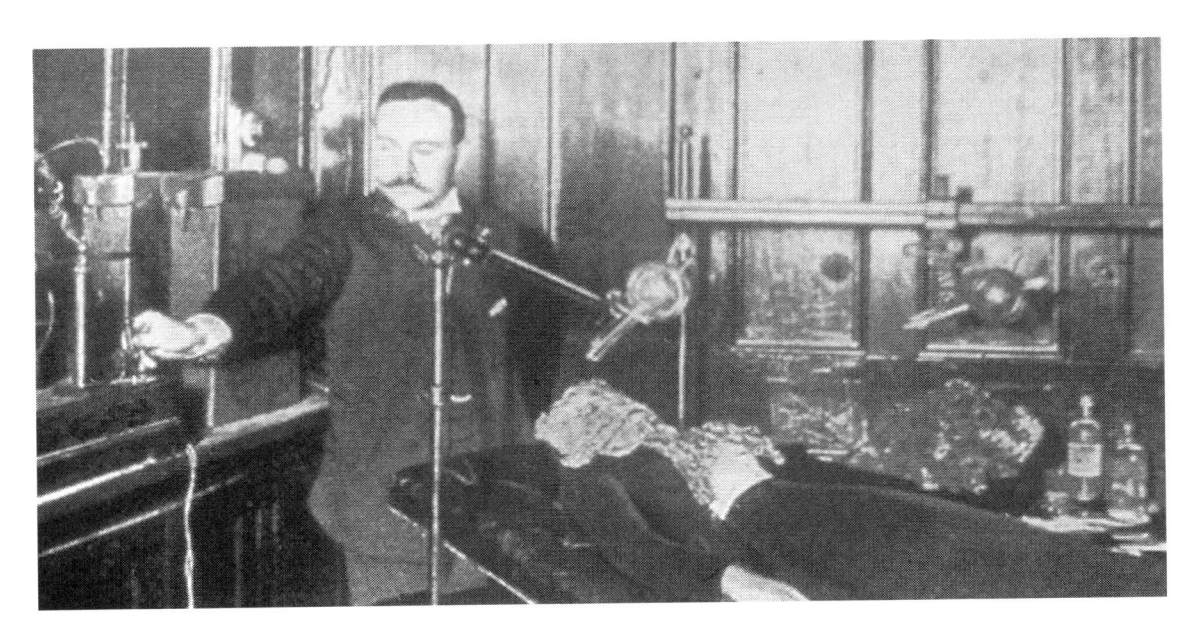

Macintyre takes a 'Skia' (X-ray). Note Vacuum Tube Above patient[9]

John Macintyre and Glasgow Royal Infirmary's early involvement in the emergent technology of X-rays was serendipitous but Macintyre saw the potential for diagnosis and treatment using X-rays and placed GRI at the forefront of the technology at the end of the 19th Century.[10] A significant factor in the early development of the speciality may have been the early installation of mains electricity within GRI in the mid-to-late 19th Century and this could well have been at Macintyre's insistence. While it is easy to belittle the early images produced with an adapted Crookes tube and basic photographic equipment, technology has relentlessly moved us beyond any of the dreams of these early pioneers in providing CT scanning and other modalities for imaging the human body. We can all, however, be grateful for Macintyre's original vision which firmly established GRI and himself within the pantheon of radiological history.

John Macintyre plaque at GRI[12]

John Macintyre died in 1928.[11]

References

[1]. Scottish Society of the History of Medicine, 1994/96
http://sshm.ac.uk/wp-content/uploads/2013/10/PROCEEDINGS-SESSION-1994-1995-and-1995-1996.pdf

[2] John Macintyre. Demonstration on the Röntgen Rays. Glasgow Med J, 1896;45(4):277-281.
https://www.ncbi.nlm.nih.gov/pmc/articles/PMC5950473/pdf/glasgowmedj5316-0037.pdf

[3]. Images courtesy of Andrew McAinsh and the Royal College of Physicians of Glasgow archive, 2018.

[4] John Macintyre. Some Notes on the Use of the Electric light in Medicine. Glasgow Med J 1885; 23 (1): 17-24.
https://www.ncbi.nlm.nih.gov/pmc/articles/PMC5913198/

[5] John Macintyre. The New Electric Pavilion of the Glasgow Royal Infirmary. Glasgow Med J, 1902;58930:161-170.
https://www.ncbi.nlm.nih.gov/pmc/articles/PMC5936316/

[6]. John Macintyre. New Medical Electrical Department of the Glasgow Royal Infirmary. Glas Med J.1914; 82(4): 263-276.

[7] Images courtesy of Alistair Tough, Archive Department, Mitchell Library, Glasgow, 2018

[8]. John Macintyre. The Modern Developments of Radium and X-ray Therapeutics. Glas Med J. 1917, 87 (5); 257-282.

[9]. Image courtesy of Alistair Forrester and the Glasgow Royal Infirmary archive

[10] The History of Radiology in Scotland, 1896-2000. Calder, J F, Edinburgh, UK:Dunedin Academic Press, 2001.

[11]. John Macintyre obituary. Glasgow Medical Journal, 1928. Vol 110, pages 363-367

[12]. Image courtesy of Craig Richardson and the Department of Medical Illustration, GRI.

Chapter 10

Redevelopment at Last

The surgical and radiological revolutions in patient care highlighted the unsuitability of the GRI estate for the Board of GRI. Patient accommodation in the Adam Block was lacking many of the basic hygiene facilities expected of the late Victorian era. More space for the new electrical technology called Skiagraphy (Radiology after 1916) had to be found given the recent advances in diagnosis. Theatres too needed upgrading to provide equipment for sterilisation and better facilities for hand and arm washing for staff.

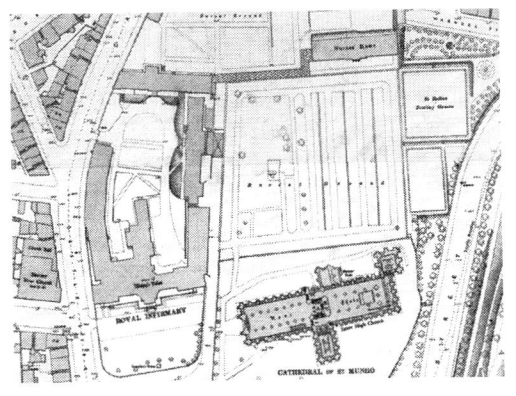

Plan of GRI and Nurses Home 1892[1]

The Schaw Auxiliary Hospital, Bearsden

Developments began in 1891 on a modest scale while the Board were wrestling with the problems of over-occupancy of beds in the GRI proper. Miss **Marjory Shanks Schaw**, a local benefactor, persuaded them of the merits of her solution by outlining her vision of a convalescent home for GRI patients from the routine wards who were almost ready for discharge to their homes. Miss Schaw eagerly agreed to

James Miller ARSA[1]

purchase a site in Bearsden, a suburb of Glasgow, to build the home and to provide generously for running costs. The Home was to be called the Schaw Convalescent Home in memory of Miss Schaw's brother. An impressive 3 storey building in the Gothic style opened in 1895 and soon became a landmark in Bearsden. Staffed by doctors and nurses from GRI, it became an auxiliary hospital for patients evacuated from GRI during World War 2. In 1948, the Schaw Home was absorbed into the NHS and became a hospital for the elderly.

The Schaw Home, while welcome, did not materially impact upon the deteriorating GRI buildings and Estate. The Lord Provost of Glasgow, Mr **David Richmond**, had no problem therefore in persuading the Hospital Board in 1897 to commemorate the 60th Anniversary Year of the reign of Queen Victoria by replacing the historic block built by the Adam brothers with a modern building. The first stage began in 1897 with the

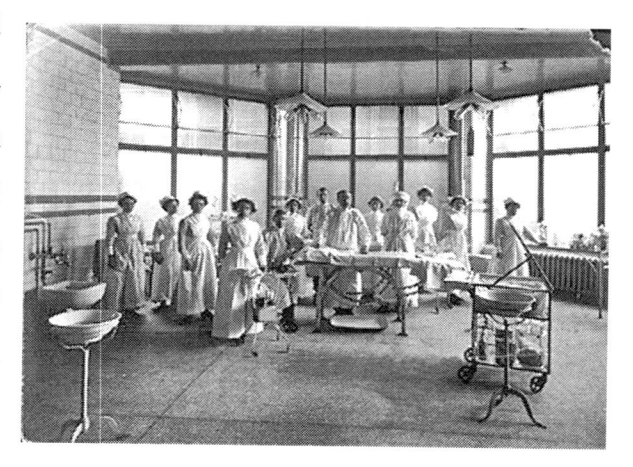

Theatre in Lister block 1914 with Dick Block behind through windows[2]

Plaque on 2nd floor Surgical to Marjory S Schaw

planning for a new 6 floor modern Surgical Block designed by **James Miller** ARSA, FRIBA who had been the architect for the 1901 Exhibition in Kelvingrove. The new building was constructed north and behind the old Lister surgical block and this required the exhumation of around 5,000 bodies from the 1849 cholera epidemic pit situated behind Lister's ward 24. The remains were re-interred at Sighthill cemetery in 1905. The Prince of Wales eventually laid the Foundation Stone in 1907. The building was called the **Robert** and **James Dick** block in grateful recognition of the

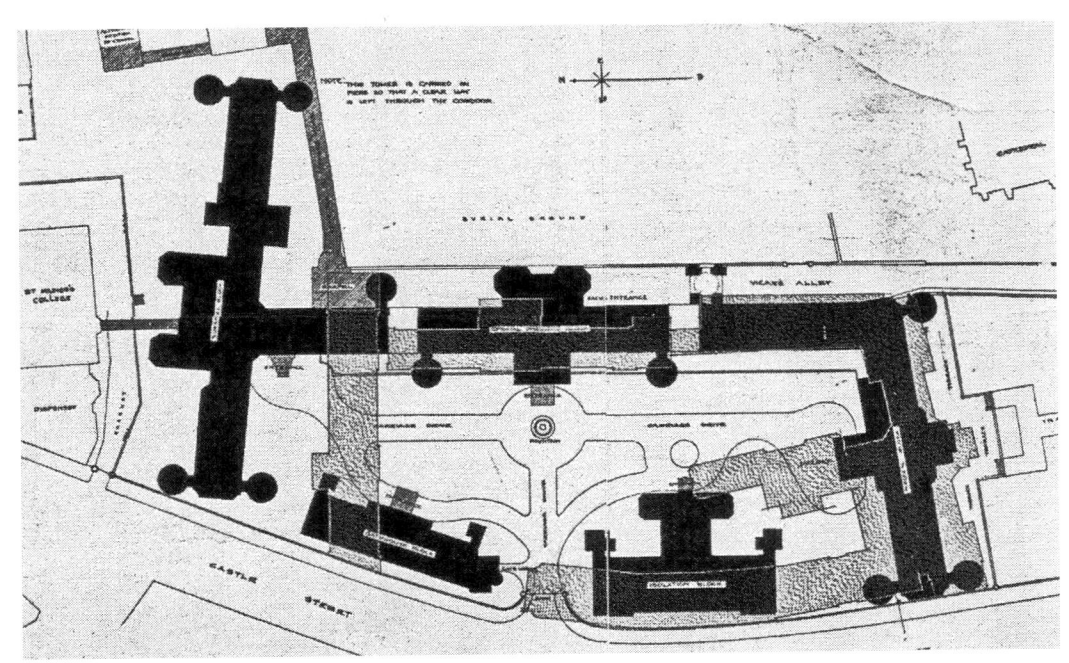

James Miller Block Plan of GRI Showing both Original and Proposed Buildings[3]

The New Admission Block, 1909, which became the 'Casualty Dpt'[3]

financial gifting of the Dick family to the £500,000 cost of building. It was opened to patients in 1909. Other significant gifting for the surgical block was from the Trustees of Miss **Marjorie S Schaw** who endowed the three, second floor wards

117

of this block as the Schaw Floor. The Dispensary and Admission Block on the West of the courtyard also opened that year with underground access to the surgical and medical ward blocks for patients requiring admission by trolley.

Entrance to Centre Block (Templeton)

This Block eventually became the Gatehouse, then the Casualty Department. A new Pathology Department followed situated behind the Nurse's Home and then in 1912, the Special Diseases and Administration Block designed by Miller opened as the Templeton Block in recognition of the gift from the local carpet manufacturer of Bridgeton on Glasgow Green. This distinctive administrative and specialist block which was the largest of the three, was built

Glasgow Royal Infirmary Crest in the 'Star'

to a different specification and had a rectangular turreted central entrance tower compared with the dome of the Medical block. Inside was a central circular 'well' with stairs to each floor at the rear. The ground floor had an arcade feel with Scottish 17th Century detailing and terrazzo marble flooring.

The 'Star' stairwell in Centre Block[3]

There was a symmetrical multipoint star in the centre of the well and the crest of the GRI was set within the marble. '**Auspice Caelo**', meaning in English, '**Favoured by Heaven**'. The resident Medical Superintendent had a flat on the top floor of Centre Block while the Matron's apartment was in the nearby Nurses Home. The Superintendent's apartment was large and eventually became the consultant's dining room when the requirement to live-in was lifted. This dining room closed in the early 1980s in favour of a communal canteen.

Demolition of Adam Block begins 1911[1]

Finally and many years after Queen Victoria's Jubilee of 1897, Miller designed the 6 floor Jubilee Medical Block with a basement and an extra floor providing for 5 Medical Units. He cleverly reproduced features from the Adam scheme including the dome and supervised it's building. Miller noted that on demolition, 'The Auld Hoose' revealed many of the compromises that the Adam brothers had to make to build it within

Queen Victoria above entrance to Jubilee Medical Block[3]

119

budget. In particular, extensive use of wood that deteriorates faster than stone made the complete rebuild timely indeed. The Board decided not to replicate the clock on the South face of the building after a trial of a dummy clock in situ. This was because it occluded a window in the Matron's accommodation under the

The New Queen Victoria Jubilee Medical Block, 1914[2]

dome. A large bronze statue of Queen Victoria by **Albert H Hodge** was placed over the South entrance and was a gift of Dr **John** and Mr **James Templeton**. King George 5th opened the new Queen Victoria Jubilee Medical Block in 1914 and the Radiology Department in the basement was called the '**King George 5th Electrical Institute**'.

The old 1860 surgical block used by Lister and comprising 120 beds remained in situ for a time within the new GRI courtyard. It was used

Demolition of Old Surgical Block from Castle Street[4]

throughout WW1 by the military for wounded soldiers and sailors and thereafter as a cloakroom for female medical students attending classes at GRI. GRI supplied 26 physicians and surgeons to the frontline in service of the military or Red Cross Hospitals. Thirty-seven nurses also served which was greatly appreciated by the military authorities.

Demolition of Lister Surgical Block. New Casualty and Admission Block on the left of Courtyard[3]

The Lister lecture theatre, North of the Admission Block, was opened in October 1928 along with two Casualty wards and a waiting room. A long campaign then began in Glasgow and furth of Glasgow to have one of Lister's wards preserved in honour of the man, his achievements and the hospital where surgery entered the modern era. Distinguished surgeons from many continents including Kocher from Switzerland and the Mayo brothers from the USA wrote about their support for the concept. The Board had the final say, however, and the building was eventually demolished in 1925. A plaque was erected visible from Castle Street commemorating 'the surgical wards from which between 1861 and 1869, Joseph Lister, Regius Professor of Surgery in the University of Glasgow, initiated the method of antiseptic treatment'.

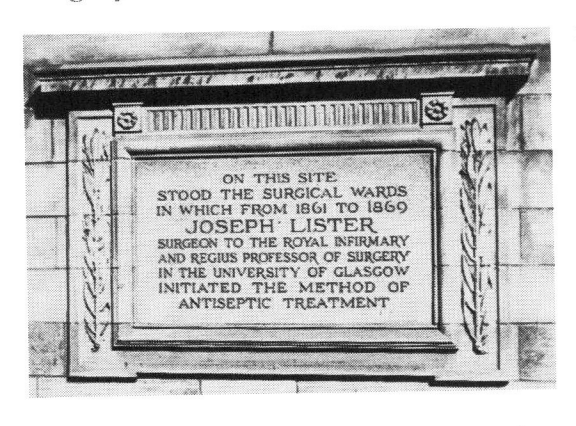

The Plaque to Lister on Castle St[3]

Lister's name will remain inextricably linked to Glasgow Royal Infirmary and Sir **Henry Wellcome**, recognising his enormous contribution, housed a reconstruction of his ward from GRI in the Wellcome Historical Medical Museum in London. Lister both initiated change and heralded even greater advances to surgical practice seen at GRI over the following 30 years through his pupil Sir William Macewen.

The continued support from the working citizens of Glasgow and from those with means remained crucial throughout the early to mid 20th Century. One unusual but very generous donation known as the **Catherine Weaver** Bequest was a Deed of Covenant providing free care at GRI for any poor Brazilian visitors or residents of Glasgow who were not subscribers. The commemoration plaque remains on first floor in the surgical (Dick) block. This bequest was arranged by **John James Weaver**, retired cashier and accountant of the City of Liverpool as a memorial to his late mother. The gift was to be used for the general purposes of the Infirmary. He was formerly of Manaos Amazonas, Brazil and his reasons were the courtesy and consideration shown during his long residence in Brazil.

Catherine Weaver Bequest

Drawing of 'new' Surgical and Centre Blocks[3]

In 1933, alarmed by the readmission rate from treated medical and surgical cases, the Board of Management came to the conclusion that social factors were indeed playing an important part in the continuation and causation of disease and permitted the appointment of the first almoner to GRI paid for by the Dorcas Society. By 1942, there were 8 fully employed GRI paid almoners to look at the environment in relation to diagnosis and treatment. They cooperated with medical staff and attempted to remove as many of the social conditions impeding recovery as possible.

The Contiguous Blind Asylum, 1901[1]

The complete building renewal in the early 20th Century set the scene for further advances in medicine and surgery by providing accommodation for patients and staff that was of high standard and flexible. For years, space for outpatients had been inadequate being usually linked to the small Dispensary and Admissions Block. In 1934, to meet the growing demand for increase in accommodation, the GRI Hospital Board acquired the ground and buildings of the contiguous Blind Asylum in Castle Street just North of the St Mungo's Medical School. In 1940, RH **John Colville**, MP, of Colville's Ltd, opened a well-appointed new outpatient Department in the converted and upgraded Asylum buildings at 106 Castle Street within the quadrangle. He also contributed to the cost. The new facility included a surgical department on ground floor, medical department on first floor, gynaecological department on second floor and was completed by an outpatient X-ray department on third floor. The five-sided clock in the iconic hexagonal steeple is

'Christ healing a blind boy' by Charles Grassby[3]

123

all that remains to this day of the Blind Institute with the sculpture of **'Christ healing a blind boy'** on the South face. An original gateway also remains that led to wards 40 – 43. This outpatient configuration continued until 1983 when the clinics re-located to the new Phase Three of the Queen Elizabeth building on Alexandra Parade. In the 1960s, cardiac surgery was placed on second floor within the existing asylum building on Castle Street. Steroid biochemistry and Biochemistry were situated on ground floor to the (R) of the entrance to the inner quadrangle. The exhaust vents of the laboratory were close to Castle Street, so there must have been mild amusement for the locals passing by to detect the aroma of the hospital.

New Outpatient Department at GRI within the Estate of the Old Blind Asylum, 1940[1]

GRI never had on-site facilities for a private nursing home which was understandable given its place in the poorer East end of Glasgow. There had been briefly a few paying beds just before the building of the North Block. But given the revenue potential that such an addition could provide, the Chairman of the Board in 1925, Mr **James Macfarlane**, later Sir James, intended to remedy this and, with his brother **George Macfarlane**, gifted land in a more affluent area of Glasgow at Canniesburn near Bearsden. A supplementary Charter was granted to GRI in 1932 to permit the building of a GRI nursing home with private beds to accompany the normal auxiliary beds for GRI used for subscribers. **James Miller**, the architect of the up-to-date GRI designed a hospital at Canniesburn in 3 blocks of two storeys, linked by a corridor. The Central block contained administration and kitchens. The East Block nearest the Switchback Road was called the **Zachary Merton** Home in recognition of a large donation from the Zachory Merton Trust and contained 80 beds with facilities for convalescent patients. The West Block was the nursing home and private wing comprising 46 single rooms, two rooms of two beds and four rooms of four beds. This Block had a separate operating theatre and X-ray Department. The Convalescent and Nursing Homes opened in 1938. The other voluntary hospital in Glasgow with private beds was the Victoria Infirmary. Designed by **Campbell Douglas** and **James Sellors**, it opened in 1888 as a voluntary hospital for the South side. James Mcfarlane of GRI probably looked on in envy as the Vic' managed to open their own private wing for paying patients designed by **John Watson, David Salmond** and **James Henry Gray**, in 1927.

Glasgow Royal Infirmary Auxiliary Hospital, Canniesburn[1]

Dispensaries in Glasgow

The term 'Dispensary[5]' had been used in Scotland to denote 'a facility where medicine is dispensed and medical advice provided free or for a very small sum' and these facilities were essential for any population in poverty. Glasgow had the lowest life expectancy of all cities in Scotland, which in turn, had the lowest life expectancy of any country in Europe. The reasons have been well described and included overcrowding in substandard living conditions, malnutrition, poor sanitation and grinding poverty. The arrival of Irish immigrants during the potato famines and people from the Highlands escaping the clearances were also significant factors.

The Scottish Dispensary Movement began in 1776 when **Andrew Duncan**, Professor of the Institutes of Medicine in Edinburgh, set up a Dispensary for the sick poor in the Capital. Supported by charities, the clinics provided teaching and experience for medical students who also offered home visitation to the needy. Charitable Dispensaries were also opened in Kelso, 1777, Dundee and Montrose, 1782 and Paisley in 1786. Glasgow was significantly behind the curve of this charitable health care movement and the health of its citizens suffered commensurately with this neglect. The city started its first Dispensary in 1794 when GRI opened its doors. The provision of free medicine must have been a real problem for the Board of Management and would have increased the running costs of the Infirmary. Waiting times and overcrowding would also have bedevilled this access to outpatient care and so the sick appeared to shun the scarce facility at first. Opposition developed to the free service from local medical men in private practice because they saw potential fees evaporate at the Dispensary door. There was also good evidence that some of those who could reasonably afford to pay for medical help were using the services of the GRI Dispensary free.

After the opening of GRI, other Dispensaries appeared but were bedevilled by financial problems. The first Glasgow City Dispensary of 1801 lasted 15 years before closing. The Celtic Dispensary of 1837 lasted 10 years. The Western Public Dispensary lasted only a few years before running out of funds. After 1850, there appear to have been more than 16 separate Dispensaries in the City[5] excluding those attached to the main voluntary hospitals, namely GRI, Western Infirmary and the Victoria Infirmary. Many of them were specialised and run by Local Authorities or charities[6]. There was a Dispensary for Ear, Nose and Throat problems, which opened for treatment of patients in 1872, and became the Glasgow Ear, Nose and Throat Hospital in 1905. The Dispensary for problems of the eye opened in 1824 followed by the Glasgow Ophthalmic Institute in 1868 at West Regent Street 'for the treatment of diseases and injuries of the eye in the afflicted poor'. Most of the work was outpatient consultation and clinical teaching. Between 1892 and 1948, it was administered by GRI but had separate funding. The Glasgow Eye Infirmary opened in 1874 at Berkely Street with 100 beds. The Glasgow Hospital and Dispensary for Diseases of the Skin appeared in 1861. The Dispensary of the Glasgow Cancer and Skin Institution opened in 1890 and after reconstruction by **James Munro and Sons**, the Glasgow Cancer Hospital emerged in the same year as the first cancer hospital in Scotland. **Princess Louise** opened this new hospital and it was soon granted a Royal Charter. Sir **George Thomas Beatson**, surgeon, became director in 1912. In 1886, the first hospital and Dispensary for women's diseases opened with 3 beds. When Miss **Agnes Barr** of Carphin presented the hospital with **property for an additional** Dispensary, the Samaritan Hospital for Women was designed in 1895 by **MacWhannel** and **Rogerson** and built in red sandstone with Scottish Baronial and Art Nouveau elements. The Royal Charter for the Samaritan Hospital for Women was granted in 1907.

The Royal Samaritan Hospital for Women

The Hospital for Sick Children, funded by charities, appeared in 1883 and was followed by the opening of their Dispensary in 1888[7]. Treatment, of course, was free if the children were poor or sick. Hot food was provided in cold weather and festive meals at Christmas. Royal patronage for the Hospital followed in

1889. Some of the Dispensaries like the Anderston Health Dispensary, the Royal Hospital for Sick Children Dispensary and the Dispensaries of the Glasgow Medical Missionary Society would also visit individuals in their own home for no charge. Apparently, there were more than one million total attendances to all Dispensaries made in 1934 and this probably reflected the lack of National Insurance or active sick club membership of the majority of unemployed, elderly, women and children in Glasgow.

Dispensary for the Royal Hospital for Sick Children

Many other changes occurred within the hospital provision for Glasgow when the Glasgow City Council was given more responsibility for public health in 1867. They were at last permitted to charge a 'poor rate' from the citizens of Glasgow to use for poor relief and Dr **James Burn Russell** became the first Medical Officer of Health of the City. He had experience at GRI, the City Poorhouse and he had been Superintendent of the Glasgow Fever Hospital at Belvidere. Welcome reforms instigated by him included improved sanitation, pollution control, slum clearances and compulsory notification of infectious disease. The Council also established a network of large

The Glasgow Medical Missionary Society Dispensary

hospitals throughout the City to care for their impoverished residents. Parliamentary Road Fever Hospital was built as a temporary stopgap in 1865 until Belvidere Fever Hospital, designed by **John Carrick**, the City Architect, opened in 1874. The Parliamentary Road Hospital was demolished when Ruchill Fever Hospital, designed by **A B MacDonald**, the City Architect, opened in 1900. Despite the capacity of the combined GRI, WIG and Victoria infirmaries of more than 2000 beds, the health of the poor population of Glasgow was so dire that these hospitals were woefully inadequate to cope with the local need. In the late 19th Century, therefore, the Glasgow Corporation began a program of poor relief by building less expensive poor-law hospitals. Three separate hospitals opened in 1904. **Alfred Hessel Tiltman** designed the Eastern District Hospital (Duke Street Hospital). It departed from the former system of combining a poorhouse catering for poverty, lunacy and physical sickness to a system of treating sick poor in purpose built accommodation. There were beds for medicine, surgery, dermatology, paediatrics and maternity. For the first time in any general hospital in Scotland, there were also 22 beds for psychiatric observation. The Western District Hospital (Oakbank Hospital) also opened in 1904 as did Stobhill Hospital. Stobhill was the largest poor-law hospital in Scotland with 1,200 beds and was designed by **John Thomson** and **Robert Douglas Sandilands**. Knightswood Hospital was opened in 1877 by the burghs of Hillhead, Maryhill and Partick and became a Glasgow Corporation Hospital when city boundaries widened in 1912. On the South side, the Govan Poorhouse had been built in 1852 to replace a cavalry barracks. It was replaced in 1867 by better accommodation then transformed by **James Thomson**, architect, into a poor-law hospital in 1923 and renamed the Southern General Hospital.

Specialised care for pregnant and non-pregnant women in Glasgow originated in 1834 with the Lying-in Hospital and Dispensary in the old Grammar School in Greyfriars Wynd. After a move to St Andrews Square in 1841 for 40 years, it

Glasgow Maternity Hospital, 1881

The Royal Maternity Hospital, Rottenrow, 1908[8]

opened with a design by **Robert Baldie** as the only Glasgow Maternity Hospital in 1881. On 10 April 1888, in an improvised surgical theatre in the top floor of this rather small hospital on Portland Street and Rottenrow, **Prof Murdoch Cameron**, the Regius Professor of Obstetrics, carried out the first successful Caesarean Section. His patient, **Catherine Colquhoun**, was affected by rickets. As an undergraduate, Murdoch Cameron had worked as a student dresser for Joseph Lister at GRI. The hospital was massively extended in 1908 with a design by **R A Bryden** and became The Maternity and Woman's Hospital of Glasgow at Rottenrow. In 1914, a Royal Charter was granted making it 'The Glasgow Royal Maternity and Woman's Hospital', affectionately known as 'The Mat' or just 'Rottenrow'.[8]

The numerous Sanitaria and Psychiatric Hospitals in Greater Glasgow have not been considered in this brief account of hospital development in the City at the end of the Victorian era.

In 1935, the GRI Board agreed to take over the work of the Glasgow Central Dispensary that was, effectively, a free medical clinic where day-surgery was also undertaken. Inaugurated in 1889 and funded by the local authority, the Central Dispensary had moved to the old Anderson's College Dispensary in Richmond Street in 1912. It was not until 1940 that the transfer to GRI occurred to coincide with the opening of the new GRI outpatient department in the annexed premises of the old Blind Asylum.

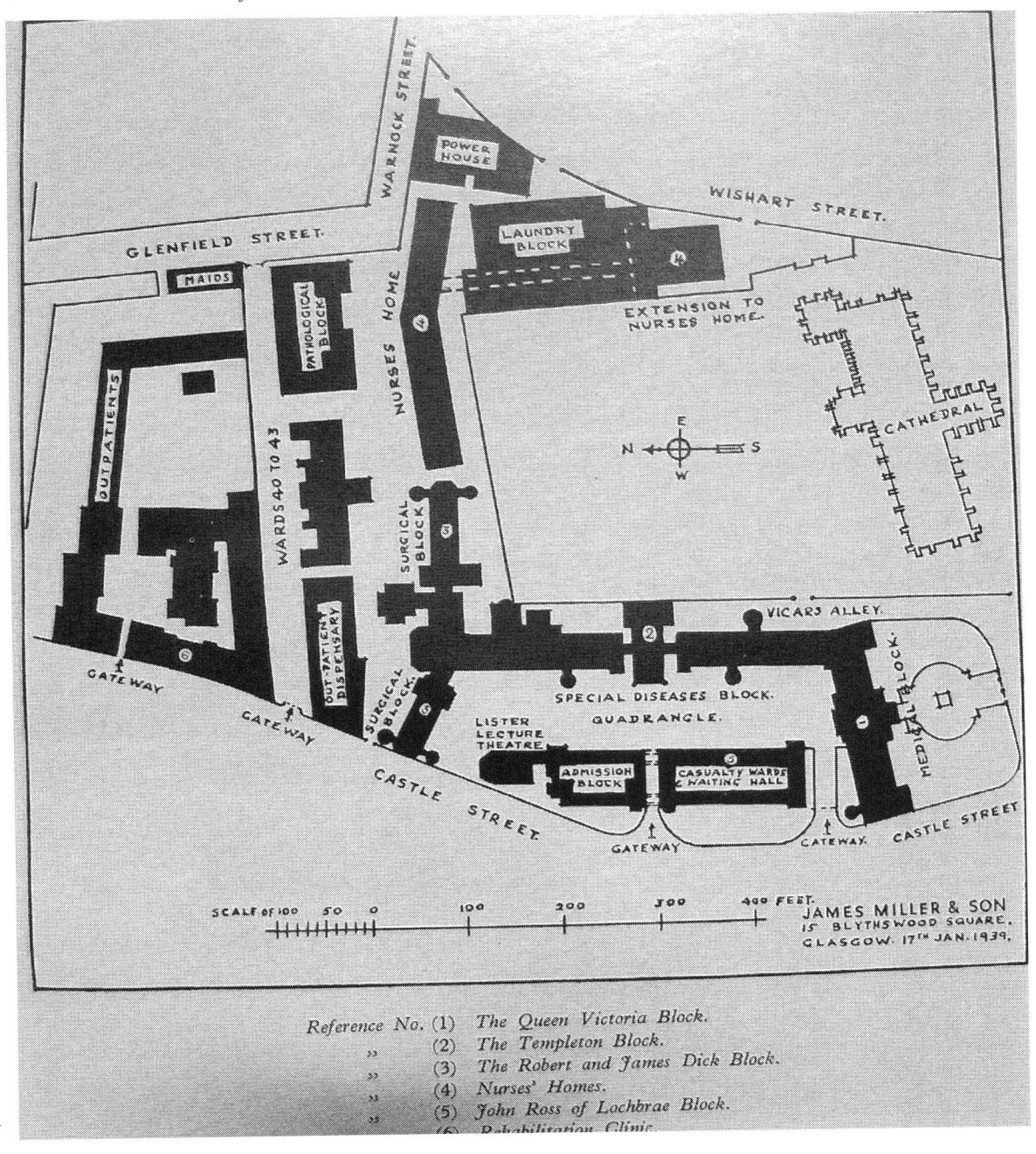

Reference No. (1) The Queen Victoria Block.
" (2) The Templeton Block.
" (3) The Robert and James Dick Block.
" (4) Nurses' Homes.
" (5) John Ross of Lochbrae Block.
" (6) Rehabilitation Clinic.

Glasgow Royal Infirmary Estate, 1939[3]

James Miller and Son helpfully sketched the Glasgow Royal Infirmary estate in 1939 so that firm of architects may have been involved in the conversion of buildings of the old Blind Asylum for use by GRI. This sketch, shown above, shows the new outpatient department within the recently purchased Blind Asylum.

Finally, it is never quite clear to the watchful observer why the University Department of Medicine on the first floor of the Jubilee Medical Block has ward numbers that are not in sequence with the other four medical units. For example, the West ward is ward 3 while the West wards of the other Units are wards 4, 6, 8

King George 5th and Queen Mary at opening of the Jubilee Medical Block 7th July, 1914[1]

and 10. The answer reflects upon a time when Royalty were not to be guided or directed even when incorrect. The original plan was for Queen Mary and King George 5th to each open a ward in the Jubilee Medical Block before King George opened the Electrical Institute in the basement. Queen Mary was asked to turn right when she walked up stairs to open ward 2 but promptly turned left and opened the East ward as the Queen Mary ward 2. King George then opened the West ward as the King George 5th ward 3. Presumably, the signs indicating the originally planned numbers had to be hastily removed.

References

[1]. Images courtesy of Alistair Tough, Archive Department, Mitchell Library, Glasgow, 2018.

[2]. Image courtesy of Andrew McAinsh and the Royal College of Physicians and Surgeons of Glasgow.

[3]. Image courtesy of Craig Richardson and the Medical Illustration Department at Glasgow Royal Infirmary.

[4]. Image courtesy of the Welcome Medical Library archive

[5]. Dispensary Services of Glasgow. A K Chalmers. BMJ: Vol 1, p289-292, 1936.

[6]. The Dispensaries: Healthcare for the Poor before the NHS. Michael Whitfield. *https://books.google.co.uk/books?id=uzwXDAAAQBAJ&printsec=frontcover&dq=isbn:1504997174&hl=en&sa=X&ved=0ahUKEwjlmv-C_ergAhWDVBUIHeewC2sQ6AEIKDAA#v=onepage&q&f=false*

[7]. The Royal Hospital for Sick Children Dispensary. *http://www.hharp.org/library/glasgow/general/dispensary.html*

[8]. The Rottenrow. The History of the Glasgow Royal Maternity Hospital, 1834-1984. Derek A Dow.

A Busy Casualty Department[1]

Chapter 11

Medicine and Management

Within years of GRI opening in the early 19th Century, the resident staff included the Medical Superintendent, Assistant Apothecary, 5 medical clerks (House Physicians), 10 surgical clerks (House Surgeons), Matron, Night Superintendent, Sisters and Nurses, Janitor, Porter, Plumber and a male nurse. By the early 20th Century, staff in residence had reduced considerably. Medical and surgical house officers slept in rooms just off the wards while Matron had her own apartment under the dome of the new Jubilee medical block. Nursing sisters and nurses-in-training lived in the new nurses home but trained nurses could stay in the community. They were not permitted to travel to GRI wearing their uniform because of infection risk. For the development of nursing, see Chapter 7.

Medical Superintendents

While the Medical Superintendent made no decisions on policy, staffing or procedures, his advice always significantly influenced the non-medical Directors on the Board of GRI. He, and he alone, had an overarching responsibility for all GRI patients and staff within the hospital and this was based both on his medical knowledge and his experience as an administrator/manager. The exercise of wisdom was required for all matters of discipline or ethics and he was the voice of GRI, the spokesperson, who related to the media and politicians. Since GRI was an independent organisation free from control by any external authority until 1947, he had significant status within the community and therefore considerable influence. In any new situation that developed, the Hospital Board of Management would normally act upon his advice. GRI has been indeed been fortunate in its choice of Medical Superintendents over the years since these individuals have each guided the Infirmary through the difficult and unpredictable circumstances found during its long history.

In 1838, the first post of Medical Superintendent was created for a **Mr Martin** who resided in a hospital-owned house, West of the Adam Building on Castle Street. He retired in 1843.

The second Medical Superintendent, Dr **Robert Scott Orr**, was an Edinburgh graduate who had responsibility for GRI during the great fever epidemic of 1847. He began the tradition of publishing statistical tables of the year's cases in the GRI Annual Report. Orr left his post in 1867 to become a visiting physician and medical teacher to GRI and by all accounts, was a well-loved physician. He became President of the Faculty of Physicians and Surgeons of Glasgow between 1880 and 1883. Dr Orr died in 1886.[3]

Robert Scott Orr[1]

The third Superintendent from 1867 to 1902 was Dr **Moses Thomas**, a graduate of Anderson's University. In 1874, he published the results of amputation cases at GRI which showed an improvement after adoption of the method of antisepsis of Lord Lister. Thomas also fully supported his surgical colleague, Sir William Macewen and Matron, Rebecca Strong in their efforts to reform nurse training. It is said that he presided at the resident's table with rigid discipline but was well liked and earned the sobriquet 'Thomas of the Royal'.[4]

Moses Thomas[2]

The fourth Superintendent from 1902 to 1925 was Dr **James Maxtone Thom OBE. D.Ph**. Thom was an Edinburgh graduate, who had spent 6 years as medical officer in the Glasgow Prisons Service. He was in post for much of the construction of the new buildings of the early 20th Century and his knowledge of architectural drawings and building methods were invaluable to the Board of Managers of GRI during this period of reconstruction. It was evidence of Thom's tact and flair for the art and craft of management that the whole reconstruction process was completed without any interruption whatsoever of the normal functioning of the Infirmary. Thom also had an engineering flair and patented a water crane that was rapidly put to use in the operating theatres. He also helped to bring in a new era of care with the National Insurance Act of 1911. Throughout World War 1, he played his part with devotion and care at personal cost to his health. Dr Thom died in 1927.[5]

James Maxtone Thom[2]

The fifth Superintendent from 1925 to 1939 was Dr **Ian Mount Grant**. He was an Edinburgh graduate who had served with distinction in World War 1 and was invalided home with the rank of Major. Under his supervision, the planning and construction of Canniesburn auxiliary hospital for convalescing patients and the GRI annex for paying patients were completed. Later he gave wise counsel during the reconstruction of the Royal Asylum for the Blind to provide a new outpatient department for GRI. Throughout, he is remembered as a dedicated servant to GRI, it's staff and interests. Dr Grant died in 1939. [6]

Ian Mount Grant[2]

Thomas (Tom) Bryson, a Glasgow graduate, was a house physician at GRI then resident obstetrician at the Royal Maternity Hospital. He was appointed Assistant Medical Superintendent of GRI in 1935 and became the sixth Medical Superintendent following the death of his predecessor in 1939. He was a devoted

Tom Bryson[2]

servant of GRI with great insight, creativity and knowledge of the workings of the large and busy Institution. Bryson had innate wisdom, which helped him to cope during the war years. Help from the citizens of Glasgow had always been required but never more so than during World War 2 when volunteer support was necessary to protect the building from shrapnel and incendiary bombs. Like all general hospitals in Glasgow, GRI was under the control of the Department of Health for Scotland which provided a contribution to running costs for air raid and service casualties. For 1941, this contribution amounted to £39,485. In fact, accidents related to the blackout were more numerous than those due to air raids.

World War 2 needed great reorganisation of medical care throughout the country. An Emergency Medical Service (EMS) was set up nationwide to receive and treat casualties with beds reserved for that purpose at the Royal and the emergency hospitals built just outside of Greater Glasgow boundaries namely Law Hospital, Lanarkshire and Killearn Hospital in Stirlingshire. Existing patients were transferred to GRI's associated hospitals at Schaw Home and Canniesburn to leave beds free for casualties. Other wartime innovations at GRI included the Burns Unit led by **Tom Gibson**, Neurosurgery led by **Sloan Robertson** and an enhanced blood bank under the National Blood Transfusion Scheme organised by **Alice Marshall** who was a pathologist at GRI. Wartime required unprecedented control by Government over administrative decisions by hospitals and this in turn provided Government with a rudimentary blueprint for a unified health service in the post war UK.

Volunteers place sandbags around GRI in 1939[1]

The Royal Infirmary was one of the national hospitals specially tasked in the early 1940s with trials of the new antibiotic penicillin which would arrive in vials of purple coloured liquid to be kept refrigerated on the wards prior to use. The first administration of penicillin at GRI was by Mr **William (Willie) Beattie** to a young man with meningococcal meningitis.[7] Against all known odds, the young man was cured and the GRI, which had led the world in antisepsis and then asepsis, entered the early antibiotic era with a drug that was effective against Gram-positive bacteria. The urine of all patients so treated would be collected for several days thereafter to permit recycling and reusing of the excreted penicillin. When commercial supplies of penicillin became available for clinical use on the 9th June 1944, 3 days after D-day, the Royal became the distribution and advisory centre for the large supplies of the antibiotic in the West of Scotland.

Penicillin core structure, where "R" is the variable group

After the war, Tom Bryson led GRI from voluntary hospital status into the new NHS in 1948. The smoothness of the transfer bears unique testimony to his energy, application and ability to work with a wide range of professions and trades. His leadership permitted GRI to assume its place as one of the largest NHS hospitals in Scotland and the UK. Dr Bryson died as a patient of GRI during 1956.[8]

James Killoch Anderson, **OBE**, a Glasgow graduate, became the seventh and final Superintendent in 1956 and is recognised as the last of the generation of doctors whose managerial role was more important than the managers appointed by the Health Board. Anderson took office at a time when Outpatients opened each morning to whoever happened to be there with a note from their General Practitioner. He was a gifted administrator, a people person, who worked closely with **George Moore**, the GRI administrator employed by the Health Board to ensure the smooth running of the large Institution. Despite the difficulties of

Killoch Anderson[9]

Killoch Anderson escorts Princess Margaret at a Tenovus Fund Raising Event, 1978[7]

the times, both economically and in labour relationships, he had the skills required to bring harmony where there was discord and showed clear leadership at all times. He was the avuncular face of GRI for the outside world and no matter who visited, Killoch Anderson made everyone feel special and at their ease.

It is also clear that his vision extended beyond GRI although he always had GRI's interests foremost in mind. In 1974, he explored mutually beneficial arrangements with groups in the nearby University of Strathclyde, which had emerged from part of Anderson's University. The original GRI had a working relationship with Anderson's University when it was at High Street and this had crystallised into a very close cooperation in medical training at the time of the St Mungo's School of Medicine. The modern GRI worked closely with the University of Strathclyde in two major research areas, one being burns, plastic surgery and prosthetics and the other, clinical pharmacology.

Thomas (Tom) Gibson, DSc, a graduate of Glasgow, worked in the Medical Research Council Burns Unit at GRI from 1942 to 1944 studying the crucial problem of infection in patients with extensive burns. Gibson was the first person to recognise that rejection of homografts was an antigen-antibody reaction. **Peter Medawar** (later Sir Peter and Nobel Laureate) came to GRI specifically to work with Gibson. Their collaboration led to the classic paper describing the 'second set' phenomenon which in 1943, laid the foundation for

Tom Gibson, President RCPSG[1]

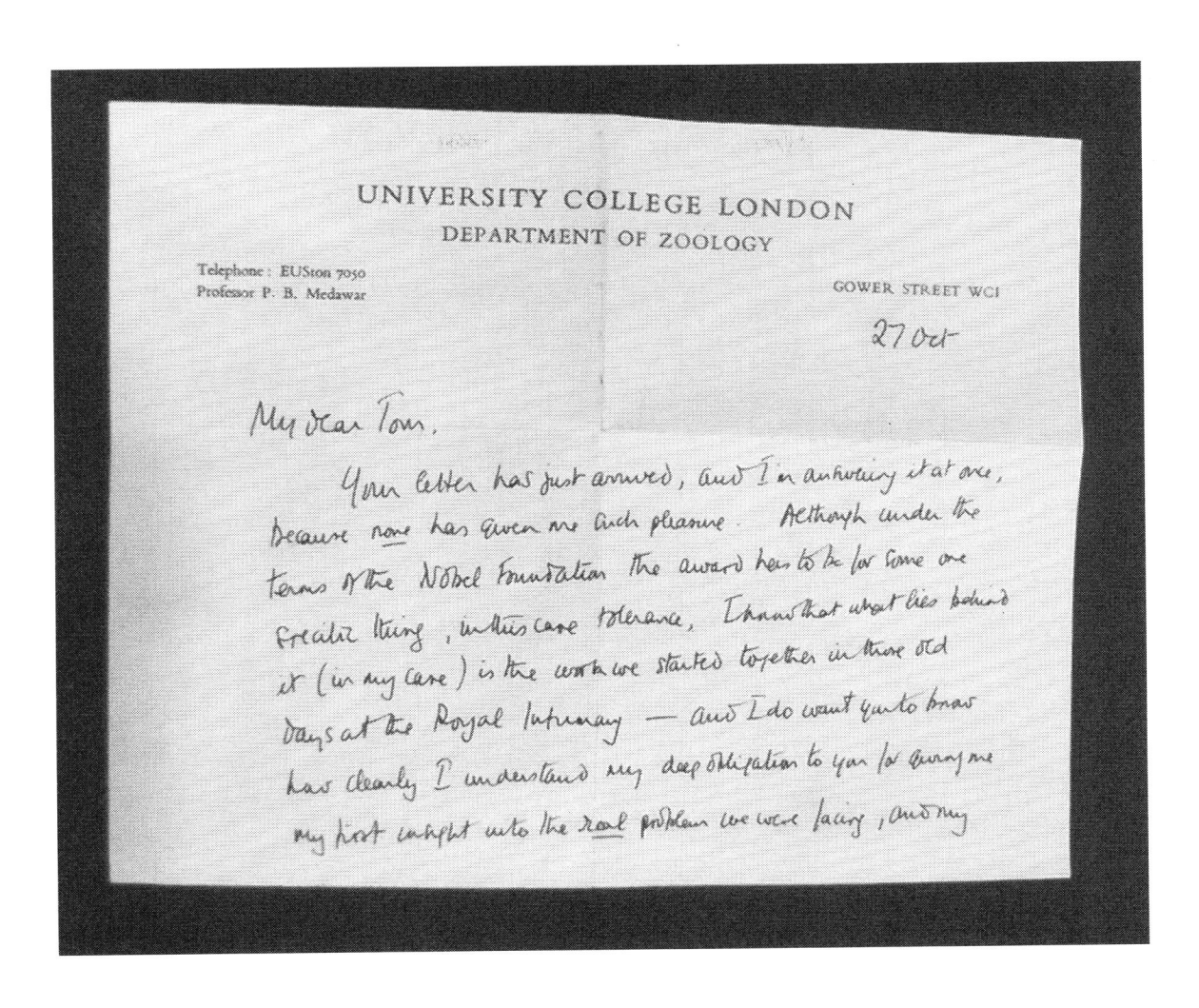

Letter to Tom Gibson from Peter Medawar[11]

tissue transplantation.[10] This phenomenon was the observation that subsequent skin grafts lasted a shorter time than the initial one. Gibson went on to establish the management of the shock phase in burns. In 1960, when Medawar received his Nobel Prize for his work on tissue rejection, he generously wrote to Gibson, recognising the importance of the work done at GRI with him. In the early 1960s, Gibson co-founded the Bioengineering Unit at the University of Strathclyde with Professor **Robert M Kenedi** and from 1970 till retiral in 1980, became Director of the West of Scotland Plastic Surgery Unit

Canniesburn Hospital for Plastic Surgery[11]

which had been founded by **Jack Tough** at Ballochmyle Hospital. Plastic Surgery moved to Canniesburn[11] Hospital in 1961 and finally to the new Jubilee building of GRI in the early 90s.

Following Killoch Anderson's discussions with the Dean of Pharmacy, Professor **Frank Fish OBE**, Professor **David H Lawson CBE. DSc**, consultant physician and clinical pharmacologist at GRI, was appointed visiting Professor attached to the University of Strathclyde. The arrangement was similar with that of Professor **Tom Gibson**, senior plastic surgeon at the GRI. Lawson eventually became Chairman of the Committee on Review of Medicines (CRM) and member of the Committee on Safety of Medicines CSM) before finally becoming Chairman of the Medicines Commission for the UK. Latterly, he was the founding Chairman of the Scottish Medicines Consortium (SMC) and was the second physician from Glasgow in 300 years to become Vice-President of The Royal College of Physicians of Edinburgh.

David H Lawson

Killoch Anderson clearly had insight that research into health matters was best done with academic co-operation and his interventions presaged a flurry of co-operative projects between doctors and scientists at GRI with the Universities of Strathclyde and Glasgow. When he retired in 1988, he had guided the Institution through the changes in local governance, consolidated links between GRI and the University of Strathclyde and had overseen the completion of Phase 1 Building in the mid 1980s. Dr Anderson died in 2002.[12]

Resident House Officers

Residents were recently qualified doctors who were attached to specific wards and assisted the visiting and non-resident senior physicians and surgeons. These senior staff are now called consultants. In the first 70 years of GRI's existence, the junior staff were called clerks but in 1862, they became physician's and surgeon's assistants. In 1888, they were renamed again as house physicians and surgeons. Their residency lasted 12 months during which time, each young doctor would assist a physician then rotate to a surgical ward spending 6 months with each. They lived in the Infirmary and received free board and lodging.

Resident Medical and Surgical House Officers have always had a stressful

Resident House Officers outside the Adam Block wearing smoking caps[2]

year in post given their relative inexperience and inevitable sleep loss. Their dining hall opened in 1880 and provided a doctor's mess for relaxation when off duty. Smoking tobacco in the late 19th Century was replaced by snooker in the early 20th Century as the favourite pastime. The opening of the mess saw the inauguration of the GRI Club with Lord Lister as its President. Members could include present and past house officers, present and past superintendents, and members of the medical and surgical staff. It provided a unique bond

Resident Charles Fyfe with nurses, surgical ward GRI, 1890[1]

of fellowship and a yearly dinner on the 2nd Friday of every March. Smoking caps were de rigueur in the late 19th Century to prevent the hair reeking of tobacco smoke and were often worn with a smoking jacket. [2] A selection of photographs of groups of resident house officers and their contemporary Medical Superintendents are shown on pages 132-134.

The relentless stress inherent in their position explains why some resident house officers misbehaved on occasion. For example, when a strict night sister was visiting wards in the surgical block in 1962 and had reached 4th floor, a dummy in nurse's uniform was hurled from the 5th floor with an accompanying scream. A shocked night sister raced down 5 flights of stairs to do what she could but when she reached the basement, there was no 'body' to be found. Needless to say, the night sister was not impressed. The Medical Superintendent, Dr Anderson, was duly informed but the culprits on this occasion were never found.[7] Insight into the conditions for residents and staff during the old hospital's existence can be obtained from the records of the Glasgow Royal Infirmary Residents Club.[13]

Traditionally, a photograph of the resident junior doctors with the Medical Superintendent was taken every six month period in the colonnade.

GRI Residents, 1929,[2] with Dr Grant and to his (L), Dr Eric G Oastler[14]

GRI Residents 1939. Dr Grant (L) and Dr Bryson Inserts [7]
See [15] for staff names

GRI residents in colonnade, 1944, with Tom Bryson [7]
See [16] for staff names

Residents in the colonnade, 1956, with Killoch Anderson lower middle.

Dr John A Thomson, co-author, top (R) [2]

The Hospital Secretary

Mr **Arthur Alexander MacIver**[2] **OBE** was the Secretary and Treasurer to the pre-NHS GRI. He worked with the Directors elected by the subscribers. MacIver also prepared the Agenda for meetings of the Directors and their committees along with the reports to be submitted. He was responsible for GRI finances and fund-raising and would have been responsible for drawing up the annual accounts.

From 1948, when funding primarily came from the taxpayer, MacIver had oversight over the funding streams from the public that remained such as legacies and donations. As the Secretary to the Board of Management for Glasgow Royal Infirmary and Associated Hospitals, he would have managed the decision making apparatus of the Board of Management and conducted

A A MacIver[9]

correspondence with the Western Regional Hospital Board on their behalf. He was awarded and OBE in 1966.

References

[1]. Images courtesy of Andrew McAinsh and the Royal College of Physicians of Glasgow archive, 2018.

[2]. Images courtesy of Alistair Tough, Archive Department, Mitchell Library, Glasgow, 2018.

[3]. Dr Robert Scott Orr obituary. The Lancet, May 22, 1886, 1001.

[4]. Dr Moses Thomas obituary. Glasgow Medical Journal, vol 76, p 27.

[5]. Dr James Maxtone Thom obituary. The British Medical Journal. April 23, 1927, 780 – 781.

[6]. Dr Ian Mount Grant obituary. The Lancet. April 1, 1939, 791.

[7]. Dr Henry W Gray, personal reflection and collection

[8]. Thomas Bryson obituary. British Medical Journal Nov 24, 1245-1246, 1956.

[9]. Image courtesy of Craig Richardson and the Medical Illustration Department at Glasgow Royal Infirmary.

[10]. The fate of skin homografts in man. Gibson T and Medawar P B
https://www.ncbi.nlm.nih.gov/pmc/articles/PMC1252734/

[11]. I.A.McGregor and R. Watson. Brit J Plastic Surgery (1998), 51, 333-342.
https://www.jprasurg.com/article/S0007-1226(96)90309-4/pdf

[12]. James Killoch Anderson obituary.
https://www.heraldscotland.com/news/11961536.Killoch_Anderson_OBE_and_former_medical_superintendent_and_voice_of_Glasgow_apos_s_Royal_Infirmary/

[13]. The Glasgow Royal Infirmary Club: List of Members, 1912. Last accessed 20th June, 2018.
https://archive.org/stream/b21463542#page/n187/search/John+F+Fergus

[14]. Dr Eric G Oastler went on to become GRI's first general endocrinologist

{15}. Inserts were Drs Grant (L) and Bryson (R). Alex Brown is back row (R). He became senior lecturer with Professor LJ Davis and became NHS Chief of 5th floor medicine at GRI. Dr Robbie Cross CBE, middle row, 4th from (L) was a fine amateur international football player in student days. He ran pathology at RAF Halton and was uncle of lead author.

[16]. Robert Walker back row (R) became consultant physician in medicine and diabetes in Lanarkshire. J Kennedy Watt is middle row, 5th from (L). He became a consultant vascular surgeon to GRI. Alex Cross is middle row, 4th from (R). He was a fine amateur international football player in student days and became a family doctor in Ballingry, Fyfe. He was the uncle of lead author. John S F Hutchison was front row, 3rd from (L) who became a consultant general surgeon at GRI.

Chapter 12

Crowd-funding 20th Century Style

By the end of the 19th Century, the income stream for GRI had become predictable though it remained quite inadequate for day-to-day running of the hospital. Personal subscriptions from the middle classes formed the bedrock of income and were most reliable. Each subscription of one Guinea (£1 1s) would permit the giver to recommend one person for admission annually and it would enable the bearer to vote at the Annual General Meeting. This would rise to two patients annually for a double subscription. The numbers of subscribers actually increased three fold between 1908 and 1941 as GRI management targeted funding from the West and South of Scotland and beyond. This was managed by use of aggressive ads in local publications and national newspapers. Personal subscriptions rose in value from £3,000 in 1830 to £13,000 in 1908 and £64,000 in 1935.

GRI Boardroom, Adam Block 1890. Names of Donors and Subscribers and amounts on wall [1]

The second of the important income streams was the total of employee contributions from local firms, mills and factories. This was slightly less than subscription income but ran a close second and was reliable except in times of unemployment. Although in work, the employee incomes were usually low making it difficult to pay the full subscription, but these workers were able to add small amounts weekly from their pay packets to the coffers of GRI and this was organised by the employer. In firms with large numbers of employees, this could amount to a significant sum. Employers were also encouraged to contribute in their own right. Depending upon their actual contributions, these employers were also permitted to recommend sick individuals annually, proportionate to their giving, on a sliding scale for £10 per year and upward. By 1907, the sum of all subscriptions (£9,310) was almost equalled by the sum contributed by all employees at £8,815. These employee contributions also provided for the workingman who supported GRI, a potential say in the running of the hospital. Each local district had an Association of Employees and from all districts, 6 delegates were appointed by ballot from these workingmen to serve as representative managers on the Annual General Court of Qualified Contributors of GRI. It was this body that had the legal duty to adopt the Report at the Annual

Employees of Colville's contribution. GRI Report, 1890[2]

Election of Worker Delegates to Board of GRI, 1926[3]

Annual GRI Delegate Meeting of Bellshill District, 1924, Bellshill Speaker[3]

General Meeting. In 1926 there were 189 delegates eligible from all areas from which six were chosen annually. This indicated considerable local interest in the running of the hospital by the workingman. The districts of the West of Scotland contained many types of business from iron works (foundries, moulders, tube works, engine works etc.), to collieries and chemical works (bleach, paint and oil works etc.). In addition, there were mills of all types (spinning, weaving etc.), glass/bottle works and distilleries. Finally, there was paper and newspaper production, office work and the agricultural industry.

GRI Income changes, 1895 Report[2]

GRI Ordinary Revenue, 1895 Report[2]

Enlisting the long-term support of these employees was crucial for the survival of the hospital and had been an insightful measure by successive treasury teams. Other sources of regular income included the Captains, crew and harbour staff from the Clyde steamers, general small donations, and church collections. Also, there was interest from stocks/shares (legacies), rents from property, the medical student's hospital/dispensary fees, and Parochial Board payments. The combination of annual subscriptions, contributions of employees in the workplaces collected by the employer, additional contribution schemes from every business, office, factory, smelter or mill in the area, and all the

THE MANAGERS OF
THE GLASGOW ROYAL INFIRMARY
EARNESTLY APPEAL FOR FUNDS.

Estimated Ordinary Expenditure This Year............ ....£90,000
Estimated Revenue:—
(1) Subscriptions and other Annual Income,..........£51,000
(2) Legacies, etc, this year,........................... 19,000
together ——— 70,000

ESTIMATED DEFICIENCY THIS YEAR,.........£20,000
MORE DONATIONS AND ANNUAL SUBSCRIPTIONS
URGENTLY REQUIRED.

Appeal for Funds. Airdrie and Coatbridge Advertiser 1918[3]

other sources provided nearly 70% of day-to-day running costs. This then represented the ordinary or predictable revenue. Each year, the treasurer of GRI, with the cashier and his team would have to facilitate the generation of the 30% of funds required for solvency and to prevent the draining of liquid reserves that was such an important legal requirement. Some years were more difficult than others and 1926 was particularly difficult due to the strikes, lockouts and high rates of unemployment. Appeals to prevent starvation in the mining community in particular in that year took away large charitable donations that would have been destined for the GRI and other voluntary hospitals.

Apart from word of mouth that was notoriously inefficient, the printed word represented the main method of mass communication among the population before the appearance of wireless. Telegraph networks facilitated overnight news reporting and improvements in wood pulp papermaking reduced the cost of the daily paper. Developments in printing technology and increased literacy among the population also helped to expand the target population. There were newspapers in every town, newsagents at every corner, and most catered for the workingman at a

Glasgow Royal Infirmary

The Infirmary was originally opened 138 years ago. It was extended from time to time to meet the demands on its accommodation. It has now been entirely reconstructed and has accommodation for 800 beds. Last year (1932) there was as many as 885 in-patients in the Infirmary at one time, and in addition there were treated at the dispensaries an average weekly number of 7,410. If the medical and nursing staffs and other officials be added, the total would represent the population of many a town.

The average length of stay in hospital of each in-patient is about 17 days, and the average cost is about £5 each. The cost of running the entire Infirmary for one day is about £290, or say 4/2 per minute.

The fact should not be lost sight of that patients from all districts in Scotland are treated free of cost, and that the Infirmary is one of the best and most widely known training centres for doctors and nurses.

In view of the increasing demands on the Infirmary and the heavy cost of maintenance, the managers hope that a liberal response will be made to the appeal of the local ladies and gentlemen who are generously giving their services in the good work.

Funding Request, Milngavie and Bearden Herald, 1933[3]

time of great change in society. Apparently, over two thirds of the population read a newspaper every day with most taking one on Sunday. Most were tabloids and the broadsheets, as today, were found in the cities. After use, families recycled newspapers for sanitary, ignition or special insulation purposes. Management used advertisements in multiple newspapers in the West of Scotland to inform the local citizens of Annual Meetings and report on special donations such as legacies. Advertisements were also placed to thank the readership for their efforts on GRI's behalf and to exhort the whole population for contributions at times of difficulty. Funding appeals for GRI in particular were a regular feature in the media throughout the West of Scotland. These were essential when rebuilding had to be funded or the new build of the satellite auxiliary hospital at Canniesburn was underway. The vast majority of these titles remain in the West of Scotland and include the 'Motherwell Times', the 'Bellshill Speaker', the 'Kirkintilloch Herald', the 'Alloa Advertiser', now the 'Alloa and Hillfoot Advertiser', the 'Falkirk Herald', the 'Bearsden and Milngavie Herald' and many more.

Managers for Election. Kirkintilloch Gazette, 1929[3]

Successful Reconstruction Appeal, The Scotsman, 1909[3]

Funding appeals generated what was called **'extraordinary income'** for the hospital. This was less predictable than **'ordinary income'**, requiring more creativity from the treasury team, more physical effort from the boots on the

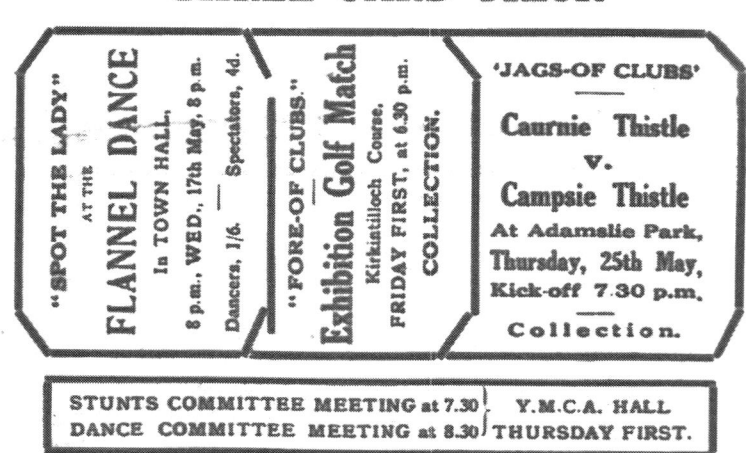

GRI Charities Day, 1933, Kirkintilloch Herald[3]

ground and more ingenuity to collect securely without loss. One weekend a year, the Student Charity Day permitted Glaswegians to contribute to all the voluntary hospitals. This included students in the streets in fancy dress with collection boxes as well as more organised affairs such as ballroom dancing in the evenings in large establishments hired for the event. There were also theatrical performances in the large Glasgow theatres that might extend over several days.

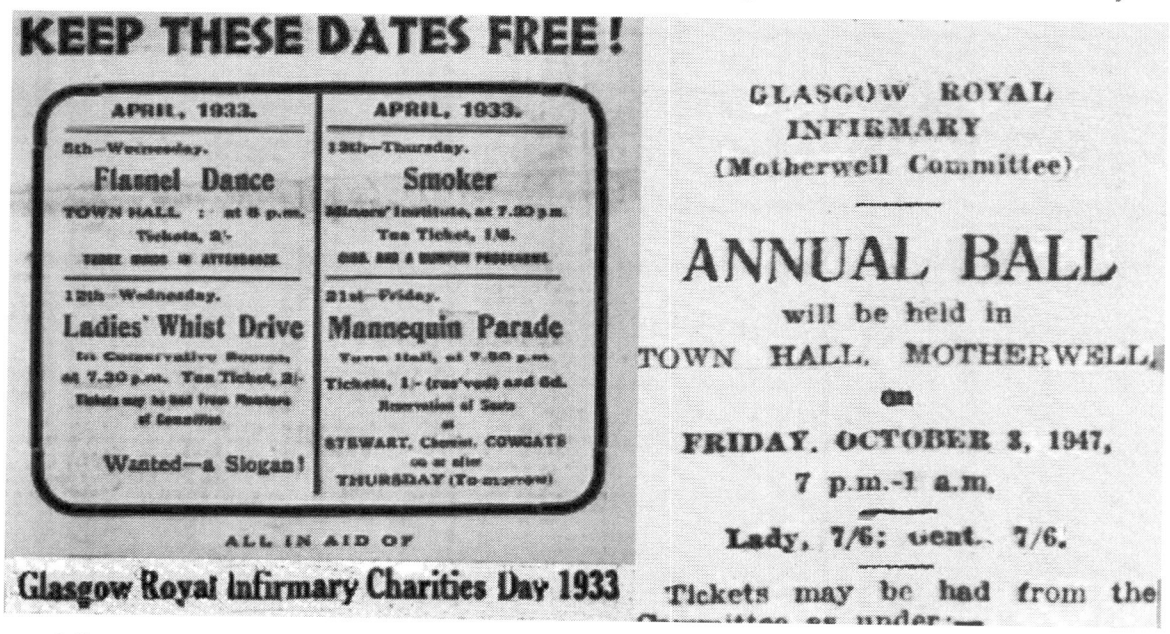

Advertisements from the Herald and Motherwell Times for student events[3]

In addition, the yearly Glasgow Royal Infirmary Flag Day was a recognised opportunity from as far away as Moray to Kirkcudbrightshire, Oban to

Kilmarnock and Lewis to Gruinard. The extent of its reach in Scotland in search of contributions made GRI the closest thing to a National Hospital. 'Have a flag in your coat, and a coin in the collectors box' was a familiar slogan in local media advertising the event. The organisation would have required a central secretariat in the treasurer's office, in central Glasgow. They also needed dedicated, trusted and committed convenors throughout the country to organise the training, encourage the young collectors for their foot slog in each district and empty the boxes safely for counting. Charities Committees were formed in most towns and areas to co-ordinate the fund raising and the mechanics of collection. The Committees for each district organised teams of Girl Guides, Scouts, Boys Brigade or other groups to carry the collection boxes around their patch. Often, Flag Days were different for different areas so this required central coordination.

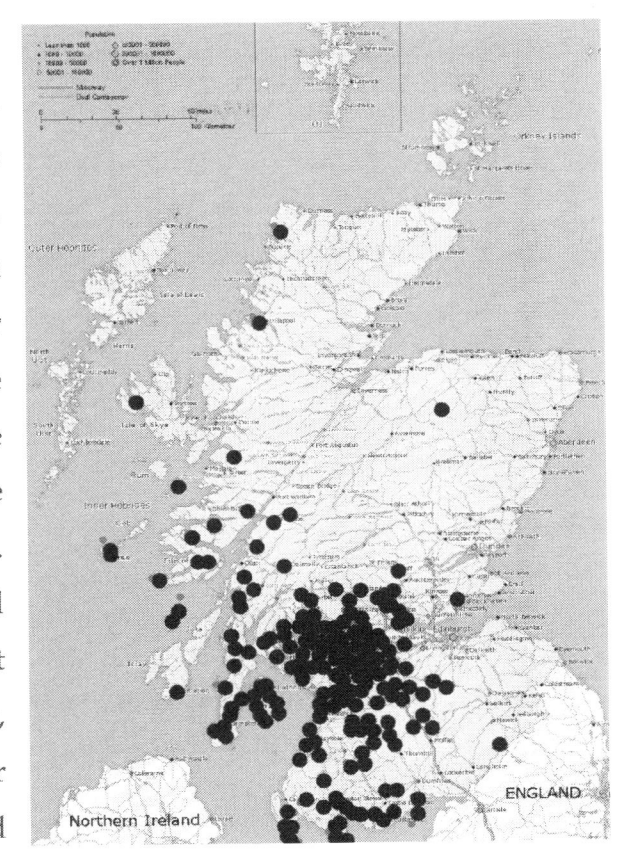

GRI Collection Centres 1930[4]

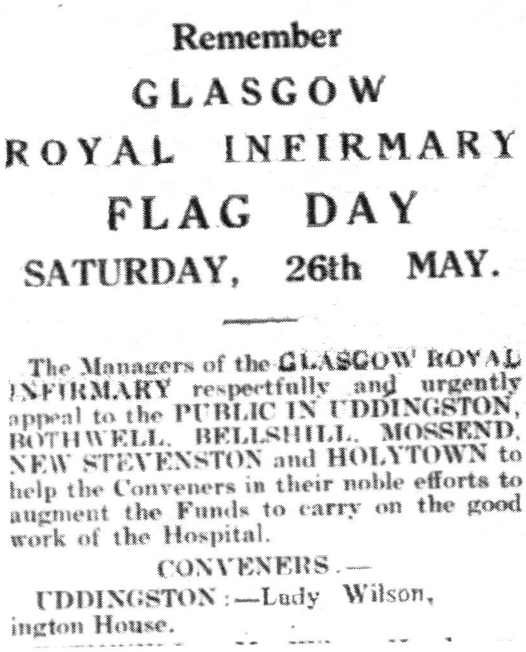

**Remember
GLASGOW
ROYAL INFIRMARY
FLAG DAY
SATURDAY, 26th MAY.**

The Managers of the GLASGOW ROYAL INFIRMARY respectfully and urgently appeal to the PUBLIC IN UDDINGSTON, BOTHWELL, BELLSHILL, MOSSEND, NEW STEVENSTON and HOLYTOWN to help the Conveners in their noble efforts to augment the Funds to carry on the good work of the Hospital.
CONVENERS.—
UDDINGSTON:—Lady Wilson, ington House.

GRI Flag Day 1923, Bellshill Speaker[3]

The task of maintaining solvency for GRI was difficult but not only because health care was expensive. The other reason was the open-door policy for outpatients and immediate admission for emergencies or accident cases without charge. In 1936, there were 375,234

155

> **Glasgow Royal Infirmary.**
>
> An authorised flag-day collection will take place on Saturday first on behalf of Glasgow Royal Infirmary in Lenzie, Auchinloch and Cadder.
>
> Glasgow Royal Infirmary is the largest voluntary hospital in the West of Scotland, while its scientific, medical and surgical equipment is of the most modern and complete description. This Infirmary annually treats patients from practically every county, town and parish in the West of Scotland. In 1936 the number of patients treated was 375,234, at an average daily expenditure of no less a sum than £324. The deficit on ordinary account at 31st December, 1936, stood at £24,459 10/9.
>
> To meet the growing need of increased accommodation the premises of the Royal Glasgow Asylum for the Blind in Castle Street have recently been purchased, and the new Auxiliary Hospital and Convalescent Home at Canniesburn, near Bearsden, will, it is hoped, be completed in the late summer. These two efforts will notably enhance the value of the Glasgow Royal Infirmary to all those requiring and using its services, but an increase in expenditure must of necessity be faced. The Glasgow Royal Infirmary has kept an "open

Flag Day Lenzie for expansion, Kirkintilloch Herald, 1936[3]

patients treated at an average daily cost of £324. At that time, there were supposedly 800 beds in GRI but at any instant, there were likely to be upwards of 885 inpatients present in all the wards. Inevitably, there were many years when the ordinary account was in deficit and 1936 did end with a deficit of £24,459. At this point, the use of scarce restricted or reserve funds would clearly become necessary. An urgent appeal to the supporters of GRI would be sent via all local newspapers in the West of Scotland. Glasgow, in particular, was very supportive of health related projects in the community. It was only when the population became aware of the political decision to bring all the United Kingdom voluntary hospitals into a new National Health Service (NHS) that fund raising became problematical. Of course we now know that voluntary or charitable funds are still required in the hospital service but this money is usually used for initiatives that our NHS is unable to fund in good time.

The Clyde River played its own part in the search for funding for GRI since by the turn of the Century, the competing railway

Flag Day 1934 in Quadrangle with Charles McKirkle, House Steward standing (left) and Bailie James Jeffrey to left of Minister McLeod both sitting[1]

The River Clyde, 1850[5]

companies were establishing their fleets to challenge for commercial, commuter and tourist traffic in the West of the Country. Large and small, the Clyde Steamers with general public access and ferries to the Islands participated in Steamer Flag days in the West of Scotland but particularly on the popular routes to Dunoon, Rothesay and Brodick. Public contributions from Steamer Flag days were separate from the regular contributions of the steamer's crews, engineers or harbour staff. This was a large industry for supplying the Western Isles, Inner Hebrides and multiple Islands of the West coast of Scotland with coal and provisions as well as

The River Clyde, 1900[5]

tourists and so the revenue from the large number of sailors and engineers was considerable.

Hospital Sunday Funds were collected to remind congregations of all denominations, of the good work that required their support. Each congregation might hold whist drives, sponsored bake activities, and 'bring and buy' sales in addition to specific retiral offerings for urgent requests. The advertisement for a Christmas gift of a GRI subscription was

Glasgow Herald announcement for Clyde Steamer contributions[2]

published most years and for those who could afford it, appeared to be both

157

GLASGOW ROYAL INFIRMARY.
A CHRISTMAS SUGGESTION.

1. IT COSTS 9s PER DAY TO KEEP A PATIENT UNDER TREATMENT IN THE WARDS OF THE "ROYAL."
2. YET THE PRESENT RATE OF REVENUE PER PATIENT IS EQUAL ONLY TO 4s 6d.
3. BECAUSE THE PUBLIC'S ANNUAL SUBSCRIPTIONS TO THIS GREAT AND BENEFICENT GLASGOW INSTITUTION ARE ONLY ENOUGH TO PAY HALF ITS COSTS, THERE IS AN ESTIMATED DEFICIENCY THIS YEAR OF £47,000.
4. TO ENABLE THE "ROYAL" TO PAY ITS WAY, AND CARRY ON UPON A SATISFACTORY BASIS, AT LEAST 225,000 ADDITIONAL SUBSCRIBERS OF 4s 6d PER ANNUM WOULD BE REQUIRED.
5. OR NEARLY 1,000,000 SHILLINGS!
6. YET A SHILLING IS ONLY ENOUGH TO MAINTAIN ONE PATIENT FOR SOMETHING LESS THAN 3 HOURS!
7. SHILLINGS ARE HEARTILY WELCOME, BUT SUBSCRIPTIONS TO THE "ROYAL" ON A LARGER SCALE MAY BE SUGGESTED AS A CHRISTMAS GIFT FROM THOSE WHO KNOW THE VALUE OF THAT GRAND OLD INSTITUTION, AND ITS URGENT NEEDS.

The financial year of the Infirmary ends on 31st December. Liberal contributions are urgently asked for and will be gratefully received and acknowledged by

A Christmas Suggestion, Glasgow Herald, 1920[3]

thoughtful and generous. The Trades House was always a faithful supporter of GRI through its 'Commonweal Fund' and, for example, provided a grant of £750 in 1941. One further source of income was the endowment of beds or cots, wards or groups of wards. By 1939, the endowment of cots brought in around £9,803 each year. By 1940, the endowment of a bed cost the donor £1,250 and this provided two privileges. Firstly, the person endowing the bed was given the title of Honorary Manager but without executive power and secondly, they had the privilege of 5 admissions annually. The endowment of a ward such as ward 28, the John MacFarlane ward, cost £10,000 and there were eight other wards so endowed. It is interesting that the majority were in the surgical block with only ward 5, the **John and George Anderson** ward in the Jubilee Medical Block. The endowment of a complete floor

OUR DEBT AND DUTY.
POSITION OF THE GLASGOW ROYAL INFIRMARY.
£330 PER DAY.

THAT'S WHAT IT COSTS TO RUN THE ROYAL—£10,000 PER MONTH; £14 PER HOUR; OR—TO GIVE THE HUMBLER CITIZEN WHO SUBSCRIBES HIS WELCOME MITE A FIGURE LESS ALARMING—4/6 PER MINUTE!
IT IS A PRIVILEGE TO PAY, EVEN IF IT BE FOR MINUTES ONLY, FOR THE CONTINUANCE OF A NOBLE TRUST ESTABLISHED AND BEQUEATHED TO OUR CARE, AND GENEROSITY BY OUR FOREFATHERS.
ALL INCOME FROM EVERY SOURCE HAS BEEN SPENT THIS YEAR ALREADY IN MAINTENANCE, AND BY 31st DECEMBER THERE WILL BE A
DEFICIENCY OF £7,000.

Appeal for funds. Milngavie and Bearsden Herald, 1920[3]

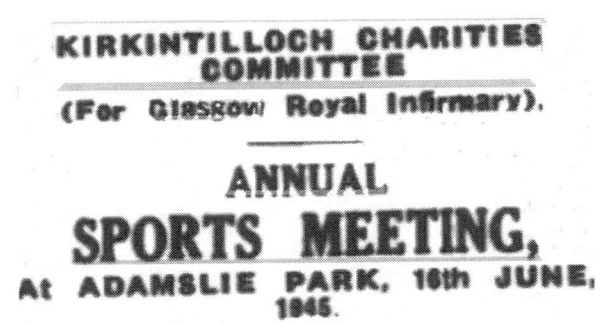

GRI Charity Event, Kirkintilloch Herald, 1945[3]

of wards was unusual but £40,000 purchased the Schaw Floor with wards 28, 29 and 30 in the Surgical Block. In 1926, the total endowment was 11 cots, 105 beds and 9 wards and there were few changes thereafter probably reflecting the difficult economic circumstances in the City.

Specific legacies, and donations from Trust Funds remained an extremely valuable income or capital resource. In 1940, GRI was left £32,321 in legacies while a year later, £28,775 was received. That year also there was £3,850 in total from special donations of under £50 for the ordinary account. The bank interest on the investment of legacies contributed £761 in 1940. Donations could also be made to GRI 'in kind' and included coal, beer, vegetables, bread and large numbers of books and toys. Each item was enumerated separately in the Annual Report and appreciation given in print. At that time during the war, it cost the GRI

Charity event supporting the voluntary hospitals in Glasgow, Glasgow Herald, 1920[3]

Management Team £500 each day to run GRI, the Schaw Home and Canniesburn Hospital.

The communication skills of the Management Teams and Treasurers were evidently superb. Information on the amounts raised by each district and a 'thank you' from the Treasurer were always published in each local or district paper for every GRI related charity event. From the early 20th Century onwards,

The 'Glasgow Herald' Appeal 1890[2]

the GRI Annual Report contained a large alphabetical list of each town and city in Scotland against the amount raised for GRI during the Flag Day and a 'thank you' again noted prominently. It remains an extraordinary triumph of management and financial control that despite the wars, economic downturns and epidemics, GRI always managed to survive, prosper and even grow as Scotland's largest voluntary hospital. In the days before internet-led crowd funding, one-off card payments, regular donations by standing order and Gift Aid, it must have been an enormous organisational behemoth for the treasurer's office and a hard slog for collectors in the streets of the West of Scotland The emphasis was clearly made that families were safer with the Institution in their midst and that their monetary sacrifice was repaid many times over by the assurance of expert help come what may. Families believed this to be true and veneration for the Institution enabled around two thirds of funding for day-to-day running in the 20th Century to be obtained by subscription and employee contributions. Glasgow was always known to be a generous city and GRI managers were also able to tap a deep well of social conscience and philanthropy among the middle classes to the advantage of the whole population of the West of Scotland. Finally, and crucially, the Institution managed to convey and inculcate a sense of responsibility and accountability for Society as a whole among the wealthy businessmen and landowners. The immortality of a family name associated with beds, wards or whole buildings appeared to be uniquely justified by the inestimable benefit to the many. While all but a few of these important names have disappeared from regular use and memory in the modern hospital, the legacy that families and individuals left to Glasgow through the Royal Infirmary has been priceless for the commonweal and represents a phenomenon sorely lacking in the Scotland of today.

A New Health Service

After the General Election of 5th July, 1945 had resulted in a Labour Government, the network of voluntary hospitals which stretched nationwide suddenly appeared redundant to the local needs as the Westminster plans were laid for a National and Comprehensive Health Service. The Board of GRI found it increasing difficult to raise the finance necessary for such a large hospital in light of an increasing reluctance of the public to fund GRI as before. It was really only the development of the National Health Service (NHS) in 1948 and the Government funding which accompanied it that brought relief

National Health Service inauguration 5th July 1948

to an intractable and existential problem. Thus ended GRI's role as a voluntary hospital reliant on the generosity of the citizens of Glasgow, the West of Scotland and of those with means. **Walter Henderson,** who was on management at the time, wrote in the last Annual Report of 1947/48 that 'contributors (financial) could be proud of the inheritance they were handing over to the State – the result of voluntary effort'. He continued that 'GRI was a lasting memorial to the warm-heartedness of the citizens of Glasgow and was a gift worthy of this "no mean city".

The introduction of the NHS certainly brought more secure funding for GRI from central government for the first time. The Management Board in the 1950s and 1960s learned quickly, however, that they now needed to compete with other hospitals for extra financial provision and this required the acquisition of new skills by the chairman – including 'realpolitik'. The subsequent explosion of medical, surgical, nursing and technical advances in the mid-to-late 20th Century would require further upgrading and rebuilding 30 years later but that would require scarce National Health Service (NHS) resources and is quite another story.

Conclusion

For over two centuries Glasgow Royal Infirmary has inspired and comforted the local population. It has also seen a significant number of distinguished and gifted individuals on it's staff who have transformed clinical practice worldwide and have provided leadership of the highest standard for other care institutions. The Infirmary has been grateful for the contributions of enumerable, devoted, yet unsung individuals in the daily round of treatment and teaching. Their gifts to the Royal have included inspiration, skills and dedication that they have provided for their generation of patients and junior staff in training. It has been said that a gift must be passed on to others or it ceases to be a gift. The same can be said about an institution like GRI. A teaching hospital first and foremost, it's doctors, nurses and, more recently, it's scientists, have each received a gift from the previous generation which they are then able to develop and pass on to the next. They, in their turn, will continue this cycle of caring,

Bicentennial Pin

Morning sun looking East from GRI[6]

teaching and researching into the future and follow in the footsteps of legions of past staff who are proud to say that they spent time at Glasgow Royal Infirmary.

In spite of the contrasting exposures to triumphs of funding (rebuilding) and to near misses (potential insolvency), GRI has managed to sustain the patient load – both in and outpatient – and maintain care of the citizens of Glasgow and the West of Scotland as the bedrock of its mission. Through intuition and creativity, advances have been initiated or absorbed which have maintained care at the cutting edge of medicine and surgery for passing on to the next generation who follow.

As the sun rises upon yet another day of caring and teaching at Glasgow Royal, one can confidently predict that its enormous contribution over the years to the health and welfare of the citizens of Glasgow and of the wider world will continue as a beacon for generations to come.

This noble quest continues.

References

[1]. Images courtesy of Andrew McAinsh and the Royal College of Physicians of Glasgow archive, 2018.

[2]. Images courtesy of Alistair Tough, Archive Department, Mitchell Library, Glasgow, 2018.

[3]. Images courtesy of the British Newspaper Archive.

[4]. Image constructed using information courtesy of Alistair Tough, Archive Department, Mitchell Library, Glasgow, 2018.

[5]. Images courtesy of Douglas Annan of Annan Photography, Glasgow.

[6]. Sunrise from Glasgow Royal Infirmary. With permission of Andrew McLaren, MSci. Photographer.

Appendix

This pipe tune march or jig for small pipes was written by George Greig after reading the proofs of this book to salute the Glasgow Royal Infirmary and the scholarship of the authors.

Glasgow Royal Infirmary

George Greig

Printed in Great Britain
by Amazon